Choral Music for Women's Voices: An Annotated Bibliography of Recommended Works

by

Charles C. Burnsworth

The Scarecrow Press, Inc.

Metuchen, N.J.   1968

Table of Contents

iv

Chapter I
The Problem and Definition of Terms Used

A new surge of interest in choral singing in America has been well under way for the past several decades, spurred chiefly by the public schools and institutions of higher learning which have fostered choral singing experience. This interest has carried over into adult, nonacademic life. Following graduation, high school choristers and college choir singers have little difficulty in finding suitable musical opportunities in community and church choirs and glee clubs.

Even within this growth, however, there is prevalent a misconception to the effect that choral groups which are comprised of either all men's or all women's voices are necessarily inferior to choral organizations of mixed voices, at least in terms of available literature, if not in their very nature.

Although the literature available to the mixed choir is more extensive, the literature for all-male or all-female groups is neither meager nor inferior. An excellent repertoire of literature is available to both men's and women's choruses. In the specific case of music for women's voices, a diligent search can uncover a great body of truly good music originally composed for high voices.

Once aware of the extent of appropriate and available literature, the conductor of a women's choir can easily achieve the same degree of enthusiasm and dedication in his group as does the conductor of the mixed choir.

I. The Problem

Statement of the problem. It was the purpose of this study (1) to give a brief account of the history of choral singing by women, (2) to establish and validate a set of criteria for selecting outstanding choral works which were originally composed for female, or high voices, (3) to annotate each work selected according to the

5

general content of its musical elements and style, (4) to provide
catalog-type information which included number of parts, range, publisher, grade of difficulty and type of accompaniment, and (5) to establish and implement a system of multiple cross indexes of those
scores examined.

Importance of the study. There has been a significant growth
within the last several decades in the number of choral organizations comprised of women's voices. With this growth, the musical
leadership of such groups has necessarily involved a great number
of men and women with only limited knowledge of the available literature. There has been a parallel increase in the number of compositions written for treble choirs by contemporary composers, as
well as the publication of previously inacessible works by earlier
composers. All of these factors underscore the urgent need for a
well-defined, selected bibliographical list.

II.   Definitions of Terms Used

Choral music. "Choral music" was interpreted to mean
part music, composed in two, three, four or more voice parts, but
not to include canons, rounds, and single melodic lines to which a
descant, or countermelody has been added.

Women's voices. The term "women's voices" has been interpreted to mean the "high" or "treble" voice parts of mature girls
or women, in contrast to the lower male voice parts commonly referred to as tenor, baritone and bass.

Women's choir. A "women's choir" was interpreted as being a choral organization of female voices, and is synonymous in
this sense with the terms "women's chorus" and "women's glee
club. "

III.   Methods Employed and Sources of Information

The information included in this study was secured by means
of examining the musical score of each work listed and, when possible, by hearing the work in actual performance. Also consulted
were articles appearing in professional journals, unpublished master's and doctoral theses, and books and essays dealing with the
topics of choral music and esthetics. Finally, the catalogs of most

major American publishing companies and the invaluable Smith College publication (compiled by Arthur W. Locke and Charles K. Fas-
set) entitled "Selected List of Choruses for Women's Voices" were
carefully screened.

IV. Delimitations

The primary purpose of this study was to examine and annotate only those works for women's voices which were scored as such
by the composer. An occasional exception has been made to include a few works originally conceived for a boys' treble choir when
both tradition and merit justify inclusion, e.g., Britten's "A Ceremony of Carols." A number of compositions originally scored for
other vocal combinations, but subsequently arranged successfully for
women's voices, have been listed but not annotated. Care was tak-
en to eliminate the large mass of transient popular music and all
other music of doubtful value. It may be assumed that each work
listed, including arrangements, has met successfully the desired
standard sought in the criteria of judgment described in Chapter
Three and is, therefore, recommended for its musical value.

Works which appear in collections, and are worthy of inclusion in this volume, are listed under the appropriate title of the
collection.

To keep the selection within reasonable limits, only those
works readily available through American publishers and distribu-
tors were considered. Finally, opera choruses and music composed
for other types of dramatic presentations were not examined in this
study.

V. Organization of the Remainder of the Study

The second chapter of this study consists of a brief history
of choral singing by women. Chapter Three details the formulation
and development of the criteria used to select the musical works included in this recommended list. Chapter Four is devoted to a descriptive annotation of the works selected. Nine items of information pertinent to each selection are included. Foremost in importance to the conductor is the descriptive annotation of each musical
composition. In the format adopted for presenting this information,

the annotation will be preceded or followed by these items: composer, title of work, publisher and catalog number, number of
voice parts and any solo assignment(s), grade of difficulty, approxi-
mate length, type of accompaniment if used, and the range from
lowest alto note to highest soprano note.

Chapter Five is a series of lists which can serve as a cross-
indexing for quick reference by conductors to all the information included in Chapter Four.   Chapter Six contains a summary and con-
clusions.

Chapter II
Women in Musical Performance

Among his many directives to the young churches of the first
century, St. Paul wrote: "Mulier tacet in ecclesia." ("Women are
silent in the churches.") (I Corinthians 14:34) This statement has
had considerable influence on female musical participation and has
led many music historians to assume that women were not allowed
to participate in musical performances until well into the eighteenth
and early nineteenth centuries. An additional speculation is that
choral groups comprised solely of women were nonexistent prior to
the nineteenth century. While it is true that this whole topic has
a vague and sparsely documented history, enough information is
available to verify that female musical performance has existed to
a significant extent from earliest times.

I. Antiquity

Drinker found historical evidence that not only were there
women musicians in Old Testament times but that they may well
have been the only musicians:

> Everything that we can deduce by working backward
> from the present to these rock paintings suggests
> that the art of music may have begun in the singing
> of music by women, and that women were the first
> musicians, and perhaps for some time the only ones![1]

There are, of course, many references to women's and girl's choruses throughout the Old Testament. As an example, Drinker
stated:

> Under King Solomon, an enthusiastic lover of music,
> the girl choirs performed in his second temple and
> also in his court orchestra. "I got me men singers
> and women singers."[2] (Ecclesiastes 2:8)

This reference suggests the equality of men and women choristers.
In some civilizations women held equal positions not only in music
but in other facets of the society, including worship rites, funeral
rites, birth rites and others. In many primitive societies women

9

performed their rites separately. "As civilization developed," wrote
Drinker, "the tendency was for men and women to carry out their
rites together."[3]

In some later civilizations or cultures, woman's role became
superior to man's. There were several pre-Christian religious sects
which had a woman as chief prophet, most notably that of Cybele,
the Great Mother of Phrygia. Her sect, although Oriental in origin,
had been established in Italy since 204 B.C. Her importance was so
great at one time that "she appeared on the coins of Antoninus Pius,
and her initiatory rite, the taurobolium, or baptism of bull's blood,
was offered for him...."[4]

Such emphasis on womanhood did not last, however, for the
role of woman in society was gradually reduced from that of equality (and the occasional situation of superiority) to a subordinate position. There may have been valid temporal reasons for this reduc-
tion, such as the necessity to emphasize and develop man's superior
physical strength for purposes of waging aggressive warfare. But
this change penetrated into matters of the spirit as well.
Drinker wrote:

> As the years passed, barriers between women
> and the affirmation of womanhood became firmly
> established. The ark, --always...a symbol of
> the womb, --remained the holy of holies for the
> Israelites, but it was guarded by men only. Wo-
> men, excluded from the priesthood, were for-
> bidden to enter the inner temple. The girl choirs
> did not sing in the most sacred place.[5]

Gradually it became evident that men had a symbol of their
own sex in God, and therefore only male officials could perform His
rites. Furthermore, "they had the sanction of the group to regard
their own activities, rites, and modes of expression as the proper
expression for all of the community.[6] Women's rites and roles soon
were either revised or distorted into worship of the male God "as
the only God".

Even Greek tragedy failed to escape this general transforma-
tion. By the time of the famous choral dramas in the fifth and fourth
centuries, B.C., the actors and the chorus were all male. According to Drinker:

> Men impersonated the women characters; only
> men and boys sang in the dramatic choruses.
> Outside of Athens, in small country commun-
> ities, women may have participated, but in
> Athens they possibly did not even attend the
> performance. [7]

By the time of the birth of Christian culture the role of women had declined to a low estate, especially that of Jewish women.
This fact had a direct bearing on how they were to be regarded in
the early days of Christianity, not only from a musical point of
view but also in relation to other churchly roles which were denied
them. It was St. Paul who

> saw through Jewish eyes the immediate solution
> to many of the social problems of his time....
> He took the lead in transmitting the prejudices
> of the ancient Jews toward women to the Chris-
> tian world then in the making. [8]

While women came to be excluded from the serious aspects of
worship, music and singing did provide at least one avenue of Christian participation and the extent of such musical participation was
greater than is generally supposed. According to Drinker, the singing of women and girls in liturgical choirs gained the sponsorship
of some of the church leaders as early as the middle of the second
century. [9] Drinker also asserts that by the middle of the fourth century, girl choirs had become "a well-established institution."[10]

The curious discrepancies that arise in the investigation of the
singing activity of women, especially in regard to the "church",
suggest that no specific policy was universally adopted within the
church. Even St. Ambrose (c. 340-97), Bishop of Milan, contributed
to these internal discrepancies. Although he shared St. Paul's view
that women should be silent in the congregation, yet at the same
time he felt they would "do well to sing their psalm."[11]

Such leading church fathers as St. Jerome, St. Augustine, St.
Zenobi, and St. Gregory of Zaziana (Nazianzus) also referred to the
choral singing of women during these early centuries. [12] The following case mentioned by Reese would seem to suggest the absence of
women singers:

> The striking diary of the pilgrimage made to

> the holy land by St. Silva (or Etheria) of Aqui-
> taine, about the year 385... mentions... the
> presence of boy choristers. [13]

But the presence of boy choristers did not preclude the use of women singers, for as Angles declares, "Boys, trained as lectors and
cantors in special schools, often alternated in the chant with men
and women...."[14] Reese's statement makes it clear that women had
an important singing role in the fourth century:

> The ascetics Flavian and Diodoros [of the Syrian
> church] are credited with having introduced...
> [antiphony] into the orthodox Christian practice
> of Antioch when, to combat the Arian heresy,
> they sought to make the services more attrac-
> tive by assigning the chanting of the psalm-
> verses to the congregation. Its members were
> divided into two semi-choruses, one of men, one
> of women and children, and the groups alternated
> with one another in the singing of the psalm-
> verses and combined in singing an Alleluia or,
> perhaps, some new refrain. [15]

Many other references to the singing of women during these
early centuries suggest that their participating role had general acceptance. Julian, for example, gave an account of a vigil of Jewish
converts to Christianity:

> The vigil is conducted on this wise. They all
> stand up in a crowd and in the midst of the
> symposium first of all two choirs are formed,
> one of men and one of women.... Then they
> sing hymns composed to the praise of God in
> many metres, and to various melodies, in one
> singing together in unison, and in another an-
> tiphonal harmonies.... Then... they mingle to-
> gether and become one choir out of two.... To
> this... the chorus of the male and female Thera-
> peutae afforded a most perfect resemblance
> with its variant and concordant melodies; and
> the sharp searching tone of the women together
> with the baritone sound of the men effected a
> harmony both symphonious and altogether mus-
> ical. [16]

Elson supported this account: "When the earliest meetings [of the
Christians] occurred in the catacombs, the female members of the
congregation took their part in singing the hymns."[17] And St. John
Chrysostom (Bishop of Constantinople, A.D. 397) described the role

of women explicitly:

> Women, too, weaving and parting the tangled
> threads with the shuttle, often sing a certain
> melody, sometimes individually and to them-
> selves, sometimes all together in concert.[18]

In another statement attributed to him, St. John Chrysostom instruct-
ed, "This I say, not only that you may yourselves sing praises, but
also that you may teach your wives and children to do so...."[19]

Yet another fourth-century Bishop, Gregory of Nyssa, described some female singing which he heard while visiting his ill sister,
Macrina. He referred to the singing of the nuns at the mourning
rite: "Virgins' voices singing psalms mingled with the lamentations
were filling the place...."[20] Women also played a part in the secular music of this same period, although records are not as plentiful as in the case of sacred music. In writing of the Roman Empire
of the late third century, Lang stated:

> The practice of music was not limited to men.
> Its vogue among women is seen in the writings
> of Lucian, who lavishes praise on the singing
> and cithara playing both of women of the aris-
> tocracy and of courtesans.[21]

Further corroboration can be found in comments by Pliny, a famous
historian, and by Lucian, an important religious teacher. The Roman historian Pliny said of his wife, Calpurnia: "She takes my verses, sets them to music, and sings them to the harp." Lucian of
Samasota, second century, described the musical customs of his
times. The musicians he mentions are almost exclusively women,
both amateur and professional.[22]

For a lengthy period after the fifth century, not much seems to
be known about the musical performance of laywomen. Presumably
they participated primarily in secular matters, although it is not
altogether certain to what extent they were active even in this realm.

The performance of sacred music by women probably declined
considerably, even within the convents and nunneries of the Middle
Ages, although it was by no means eliminated. One reason for its
decline was mentioned by Elson, who stated that the Synod of Antioch
in the year 379 abolished the custom of permitting men and women

to sing together. [23]

II. The Middle Ages

The extent of female choral participation in the Middle Ages
is difficult to document. Two major problems beset the investigator
here: first, general records of the times are either incomplete or
unobtainable, and second, those which are available contain many con-
tradictions.

E. K. Chambers, in describing a sixth-century wedding scene
during the time of Queen Guinevere, stated that "women sang....
The men shouted...."[24] Queen Guinevere is even reputed to have
composed some of the songs. But Chamber's statement does not
make it clear whether this scene was associated with the sacred
part of the wedding ceremony or the secular celebration afterwards.
On the basis of other discernible facts from this period it would
seem that the female singing had no place in the sacred ceremony.

It has been fairly well documented that public performance of
religious music by women and girls was not allowed during this
period. Drinker wrote:

> The liturgical choirs of girls, who preceded the
> boy choirs, eventually became cloistered in their
> own monasteries and no longer served in the pub-
> lic churches. Choirs of laywomen and girls, as
> well as of professional musicians, were abso-
> lutely forbidden. Congregational singing by women
> was also forbidden, even when they were in church
> with their families. [25]

The practice of using boys for treble melody parts was common. In the New Oxford History of Music Handschin stated:

> In the first Roman Ordo, a ceremonial designed
> for the papal service and probably written in the
> eighth century.... we read that in the Easter Day
> vespers an Alleluia is sung with three psalm ver-
> ses, after which an Alleluia is sung again with
> melodiae by the boys. [26]

It is probable that only in the nunneries or cloisters were women permitted to participate in religious music. Plainsong was sung
by these convent women and "became an earnest expression of their
own spiritual life."[27] Drinker described their vocal training in this
manner:

> The singing of nuns was a serious religious matter,
> sanctioned chiefly for the purpose of enhancing the
> value of prayers to the Almighty. Provisions were
> made for the singers to be properly trained. Each
> convent had its own nun-teacher. She was called
> cantrix, cantorissa, sangerin, or singmeisterin ac-
> cording to the language of her country. [28]

This last statement suggests that both the singing and the training of
the nuns were apparently widespread.

Often monasteries established for the seclusion of ascetic
monks also included quarters for nuns. How often, if ever, these
men and women combined their vocal efforts in praise of God during this early period is difficult to determine. It is certain that both
groups separately engaged in frequent and earnest musical efforts,
especially within the Benedictine order, which included among other
interests a dedication to artistic pursuits. "From the fifth century
until about the thirteenth," according to Drinker, "monks and nuns
of the Benedictine monasteries often spent from five to eight hours
daily in the practice and performance of liturgical song."[29] Such
dedication resulted in high artistic achievement, attested to by numerous references in the writings of their contemporaries throughout
the centuries.

Music, of course, was not the only field of artistic endeavor
for these nuns. During the tenth century a learned German nun,
Roswitha, produced six plays in Latin prose.[30] Smoldon suggests,
however, that there is some controversy over whether the plays
were ever performed in her own nunnery. Since this was the ap-
proximate time of the birth of liturgical drama, which normally employed music, it would seem logical to conclude that Roswitha's
plays were, in fact, liturgical dramas. Further, most evidence suggests that nuns were not permitted to perform in early liturgical
drama, thus the reason for the controversy referred to by Smoldon.
It is his belief that they did not even participate in the famous Quem
quaeritis trope which dealt with the gospel account of three women
approaching Jesus' tomb. He wrote, "Surviving rubrics tell us that
three clerics are required to robe and hood themselves as women...."[31] The denying of female participation in the liturgical

dramas may have been a common practice, as indicated by Drinker:

> Over and over again, nuns were forbidden to act
> in the liturgical plays. Women could not even re-
> produce the scene in which the three Marys visit-
> ed the holy sepulchre on Easter morning. In all
> Europe and England, the Easter drama has so far
> been found in only six monasteries for women,
> whereas in the monasteries for men the play was
> never suppressed. [32]

The performers of the Quem quaeritis trope (liturgical drama) may
have been at first limited to priests and choir boys, but as the plays
developed and became disassociated from the Mass it is quite possible that nuns were gradually included. This detaching of the trope
from the Mass and its subsequent move to the end of Easter matins
were significant developments. The liturgical drama then achieved
"a generous amount of literary freedom and developed into an authentic Easter Play,"[33] according to Young. He continues: "The move
to the end of the Matins signalized details of costume and gesture--
genuine impersonation."[34] Young's use of the terms "authentic" and
"genuine impersonation" implies the possible use of women--nuns.
Meese also observed, "About the year 1141 the places of the boy
choristers were taken by adult falsetto singers...."[35] Whether the
term "adult falsetto singers" refers to women or to male falsetto
singers is not clear. Quite probably, his reference was to a specific
community or location of performance and did not imply the use of
adult falsettos as a general practice. Undoubtedly, performance
practices varied as much as did the texts used in the various ver-
sions of this and other liturgical dramas.

   The issue of women performers in secular circles of this
period is less open to question for lack of documentation. For example, it is known that around 1050 Queen Margaret of Scotland
"was famous for the ballads she composed and sang with her ladies-
in-waiting."[36] During the ninth century the jongleurs of France and
their counterparts, the German gänkler, began to appear. According
to Reese:

> These men--and women--were often poor vagabonds
> who sang songs that others wrote, did tricks with
> trained bears or such other collaborators, animal
> or human, as might be at hand, found themselves

> especially in demand to enliven less elegant wed-
> ding festivities, behaved scandalously, and were
> in general the despair of the clergy. [37]

During a slightly later period, women were included also among the
aristocratic poet-musicians of France. Reese wrote:

> The troubadours and trouveres were not wander-
> ers like the jongleurs, but especially in the ear-
> lier years, persons of rank--noblemen, princes,
> occasionally ladies of high position. They flour-
> ished for some 200 years, from the end of the
> eleventh century to the end of the thirteenth, the
> best part of the Age of Chivalry. [38]

Included among their compositions were dramatic love ballads which
were apparently mimed, therefore necessitating the use of women.
Ritter further documents Reese's statement:

> ...a number of ladies of rank, wives, sisters or
> daughters of troubadours, generally became trou-
> veresses, as they were called. Marie de France
> and Clara d'Anduse were among the most famous
> of these. [39]

As secular female singing became even more widespread, the
church eventually had to relax some of its rigid rules on sacred lay
participation. As Drinker related:

> About the thirteenth century, one compromise was
> the introduction of congregational singing into the
> Roman Catholic Church. Religious words and fa-
> miliar tunes that had never been silenced out-of-
> doors became formalized into hymns sung at the
> high festivals of Christmas and Easter. [40]

Women no doubt engaged in this congregational singing, as they must
have participated in the responsories of the worship service. Within
a century, the church also relaxed its formal pronouncement against
secular female choral participation. Drinker detailed this evolution:

> Up to 1400 the Church had persistently refused
> to countenance anything but the high, clear sing-
> ing of the Gregorian chants by the nuns. The
> rich, natural voice of the mature woman was
> considered to be outside the pale of decency....
> But by 1400 the natural woman was coming into
> her own.... The Church was forced to yield to
> the popular will and tacitly condone the perform-
> ance of pagan music under Christian titles in the
> form of... hymns and carols.... Everywhere the
> people were singing new folk songs, popular

ditties, Christian carols, and spirituals--many
of them composed by women and girls. [41]

The medieval town was instrumental in encouraging the growth
of a strong secular community capable of influencing the local parish.
Harrison wrote:

> The medieval town [of the fourteenth century]
> was a community behind walls.... Music emerg-
> ed spontaneously, with its own style and forms,
> as an adornment of this [middle class] life and
> as the handmaid of divine worship. The home,
> the inn, the market and the street became the
> main centers of singing.... [42]

While these concessions were being made somewhat informally
by the churches, the nunneries continued to develop and encourage
female participation in the more formal manner peculiar to them.
After describing a number of manuscripts of liturgical dramas,
many of which contain parts for the Marys, Smoldon related that
"from the nunnery of Origny-Saints-Benoite [came] the fourteenth
century St. Quentin drama...."[43] The implication is not only that
women sang and portrayed these roles, but that they may even have
written the drama and the associated music. An even stronger statement was made by Reese:

> The Las Huelgas MS contains a two-part exer-
> cise in solfeggio, the text of which shows that
> the piece was intended for the nuns of the con-
> vent. Yet the customary clefs are used. From
> this fact it may be deduced that neither the
> choice of the clefs nor the apparent tessitura
> indicates that works in thirteenth (or fourteenth)
> century MSS were intended for the exclusive use
> of men's voices. The clefs were chosen with a
> view of placing all the notes on the staff, and it
> is wholly likely that motets, conducti, etc. were
> sometimes sung by women--whether as nuns in
> convents or as trained or amateur singers in
> secular life. [44]

In other words, the position of the clefs in these early works does
not necessarily indicate the voice to which the part was assigned.
It was common, whenever the normal voice range exceeded the five-
line staff, to introduce another clef or to simply alter the position
of the original clef.

Since the Benedictine order was in part dedicated to artistic pursuits, the activity of Benedictine nuns in female choral performance is significant. An interesting source of information describing their practices in the late thirteenth century is a little-known manuscript written at Barking Abbey, an ancient abbey founded about 677 and the second English monastery for nuns. Entitled The Ordinale and Customary of the Benedictine Nuns of Barking Abbey, the manuscript was presented to Sibille Felton, Abbess of Barking, in 1404.[45] In addition to detailed rubrics, the manuscript contains valuable information about choral performances at the Abbey and includes liturgical directions for the presumably all-women choir. The general scope covers antiphons, psalms, chapters, hymns, collects, invitatories and responds. Several notes provided by Dame Lamentia McLachlan, L. S. B. , shed some light on the nuns' singing. She says the singing of antiphons in the cloister is analogous to carol-singing.[46] Next she points out that the Ymeras agios sung at Barking on four festival days (Christmas, the Circumcision, the Epiphany and the Transfiguration) "was probably one of the very earliest pieces of plainsong to be harmonized."[47] Finally, she remarks that the Service of the Resurrection or of the Sepulchre,[48] a liturgical drama used at Barking Abbey, was like the Quem quaeritis in that it employed three Marys.

Even more detailed information about the choral practices of Benedictine nuns during the Middle Ages can be found in Hilpisch's History of Benedictine Nuns published in 1958. Hilpisch's comment on the significance of the chantress is as follows:

> The chantress was important: generally only one
> who had been especially trained would be chosen.
> She was not only, as today, a director of the
> choir but since there was much room for develop-
> ment in the liturgical life, she was expected to
> compose hymns and set them to music. Thus she
> had to be both poet and musician at the same
> time.[49]

This small volume makes it clear that choir singing in the convents was highly regarded not only by the singers but by those who determined the general procedures of convent life. As Hilpisch wrote:

The religious life consisted first and foremost in
the performance of choir service, which was
given particular solemnity through the procession
in the cloister and other practices. [50]

By the sixteenth century nuns were devoting a great amount of time
to singing. "The canonical hours," Hilpisch observed, "were sung
completely every day and current popular devotions were added."[51]

Parallel to this development, secular activity continued to flour-
ish. In addition to many written statements describing the role of
women in both sacred and secular music, numerous art works of
the period document the growing participation by women, not only in
vocal activity, but in instrumental music as well. A late fourteenth-
century woodcarving from the Bambury Cathedral, as an example,
shows a man playing a harp while a woman plays on a lute. The
subjects appear to be members of the aristocracy. Two other art
works showing secular activity are (1) Basano's (1510-1592) "The
Artist with His Family", which depicts a woman playing a keyboard
instrument and a woman playing a lute, along with five men and two
boys and (2) "Group of Feminine Musicians" by an unknown French
artist (c. 1520), which includes a flutist, a lutist and a singer. In
a sixteenth-century tapestry, two of the three singers depicted are
women, and the harpist included in the group is also a woman.

III. The Sixteenth Century

If the word "renaissance" can be interpreted to mean "the
liberation of music from the bondage of the Church"[52], then the
later Middle Ages may perhaps be called the beginnings of a musical
"renaissance". While, as Lang expressed it, "the monkish theology
of the early Middle Ages belittled women and considered them the
most pliable tool in the hands of Satan, [it] was left to the Renaissance to reinstate women to human society...."[53]

Although the Church gradually became more permissive, the
impetus for restoring women to musical performance was provided
primarily, as has been seen, by secular activities. Drinker related
that young girls of court families were groomed from childhood to
marry into other rich families, in order to gain power and wealth:

One hears of girls who learned Greek, Latin,
Hebrew, philosophy, theology and medicine;

> girls who read the works of Plato,... Greek
> mythology, bible history... learned to make
> tapestry and to play the harp. Above all,
> they learned to make verse and to sing and
> compose in the new contrapuntal style. [54]

While some of these young girls married into royal families,
many of their equally trained and musically gifted sisters did not,
and chose the convent as an alternative. These highly trained singers, added to those who were receiving good training in the convents, greatly improved the level of artistic performance. Though
some nuns' groups had been granted a few liberties in singing performances, the addition of members who possessed more diversified talents and interests gradually brought about more freedom. In
Cologne, in 1550, according to Drinker,

> an edict was given out by the bishop that the
> nuns might act the parts of the three Marys
> in the Easter plays. In Italy, many convents
> produced sacre rappresentazioni. [55]

Choral singing by nuns evidently achieved a reasonably good
standard of quality. Kinkeldey, for example, stated that "sacred
music for high voices was much used in convents, in some of which
the nuns often reached a high level of performance." [56] Female singing in the monastery chapels in the sixteenth century was so good,
according to Drinker, that it attracted worshipers to these chapels
instead of the regular parishes:

> At the Chiesa dello Spirito Sancto in Rome, the
> nuns sang vespers on Easter Monday with such
> perfection that the critic Pietro della Vallo said
> he had never in his life heard such beautiful
> music. [57]

Instrumental playing had also achieved a level of high repute among
the religious sisters. Lang's account relates:

> Musical organizations founded and conducted by
> women were numerous, especially in Italy, and
> the religious in almost every convent were de-
> voted to the music. They sang and played various
> instruments so well that the Venetians, Bolognese,
> Neapolitan, and Milanese public flocked to the
> evening services to hear their magnificent choral
> singing. The religious were not only engaged in
> the study and performance of sacred music but
> were skilled in all varieties of secular music. [58]

Though earlier composers may possibly have given some attention to
the convents, the growing reputation of musical excellence among
nuns aroused the interest of leading sixteenth-century composers.
As Drinker suggests:

> It was for singers such as these that Palestrina,
> Lasso, Vittoria, Monteverdi, Couperin, Lotti,
> and other famous church composers wrote motets
> to be performed at special services. [59]

David lists several specific works as possibly having been intended
for such groups, for example:

> Eleven of the twenty-one compositions of Pale-
> strina's Mottetorum quatuor vocibus partim plena
> voce at partem paribus vocibus liber secundas
> (1581) were for high voices, probably intended
> either for choir boys or for nuns. [60]

Emphasis on musical performance was increasing not only in
convents but also in other areas of devotional practice, including
the regular church service. This was due at least in part to the
secular spirit which had permeated sacred music. Masses were
frequently based on secular cantus firmi or parodied from chansons,
and the use of instruments and complicated polyphony became widespread. Secularism, however, was soon to have its influence on religious matters challenged by a violent reprimand from
high church authorities. It came as a result of the Council of Trent
in the middle of the sixteenth century and affected the choral practices of the nuns as well as church policies in general. In 1590 the
convent at Kühbach in the diocese of Augsburg received a series
of statutes directed at removing certain improprieties which had
crept into the convents. According to Hilpisch, the laws began:

> First the religious service to which according to
> the teaching of our Holy Father St. Benedict,
> nothing is to be preferred, is to be performed
> devoutly in choir and elsewhere, with propriety,
> with complete words, with long pauses, with
> distinct syllables, with uniform voice, not one
> high, another low, in singing, reading and chant-
> ing. [61]

Musical performance in general had become careless. Polyphony undoubtedly made it difficult to understand the words, which in turn

encouraged bad pronunciation, and the general attitude of the singers
was irreverent.

Despite this apparent reversal, singing by women had become
accepted by the church. The newborn Protestant churches also provided for female participation, mainly through congregational singing. The Lutheran service in its early years encouraged congregational singing, and in 1559, during Queen Elizabeth's reign in England, congregational psalm-singing was officially permitted. [62] Drinker even put forth the suggestion that there may have been Protestant
female choirs:

> In the Calvinist churches in Switzerland and France
> there may have been trained women's choirs. Goudi-
> mel, in 1565, set eight psalms for four high voices.
> In his preface to the collection he says that he com-
> posed the music for both home and church use. [63]

Toward the end of the century in England, a dramatic change
was made in the arrangement of the regular vocal parts in congregational music, which indicates that it was a widespread and quite
acceptable practice for women to sing in the congregation. According to Harman and Milner, "the Psalter of Alison, published in
1599... is important in that the tune is always placed in the soprano
part instead of the customary tenor...."[64]

Despite this impressive record of female musical endeavor
within the church, secular opportunities for women in music were
more important, plentiful and diversified. The normal pattern during
most of this century was for women to perform only with women.
According to Lang:

> In the actual performance of music, women seem
> to have been restricted to their own circle. Emi-
> nent soloists no doubt took part in madrigal sing-
> ing and other intimate performances, but the pre-
> ferred medium for alto and soprano parts was the
> boy's voice.... [65]

One exception to the general pattern was observed by Reese:

> In Part I of the Dialogo della musica (1544)
> Antonfrancesco Doni gives the music of sev-
> eral madrigals, sung by the interlocutors,
> who are four men. In Part II, seven men
> and one woman sing compositions in varying
> numbers of parts. [66]

This is one of the rare references to joint male and female participation.

Women at this time also reached independent stature as musicians and several gained high fame. Chief among them was Isabelle
d'Este, whom Lang describes as "the most accomplished [female]
figure, the perfect dilettante, the very donna universale of the Renaissance ideal...."[67] Other women also came into prominence, as
noted by Reese:

> In 1583 Giaches de Wert began his visits to Fer-
> rara. Here he fell in love with Targuinia Molza,
> who, with Laura Peperara and Lucrezia Bendidio,
> took part in celebrated concerts of women per-
> formers at the court of the Este. Targuinia was
> composer, conductor, singer and instrumentalist
> in the court....[68]

In a significant account, Harman and Milner mentioned the same
three women:

> The fame of these three [ladies] spread far be-
> yond Ferrara and even beyond Italy, and Alfonso,
> [II, head of the Ferrarese court 1558-1597] fully
> aware of this and knowing that attempts had been
> made to find out what kind of music they sang
> and how they sang it, forbade the publication of
> their repertoire.... Among the numerous com-
> posers who paid homage to the three ladies was
> Claudio Monteverdi.[69]

Interest in instrumental playing by women, which began in the
fourteenth and fifteenth centuries, was also growing. Reese stated:

> The thousands of pilgrims who came to Cologne
> annually from all along the Rhine early in the
> sixteenth century included musicians.... Among
> the several female singers named in contempor-
> ary records are some who also played instru-
> ments.[70]

At least three other prominent women musicians were listed by
Drinker as "Lucrezia Tuornabuoni [who] composed Christmas
carols... Margaret of Austria [who] made beautiful love songs [and]
Anne Boleyn [who] could dance and sing [and] play the lute."[71]
Among women composers of this period, listed by Elson were Mad-
dalena Caulana, who published two volumes of madrigals in 1568 and
1583; Vittoria Alcotti, who published Chirlanda dei Madrigali a 4

voci in 1593; and Francesca Caccini (b. 1581), who was the daughter
of the famed Florentine and who possessed a great singing and composing talent. [72]

Women composers of a slightly later era whom Elson included
were Barbara Strozzi, who had an opera produced in Venice in 1695;
Cattarina Assandra (c. 1600), who wrote a two voice Veni Sancte
Spiritus; and Cornelia Calegari (b. 1644), who sang, played organ
motets at the age of fifteen and wrote several masses for six voices
and instruments. [73]

Among works specifically written for women, Hans David cites
Louange et gloire by Henry Lecouteux as one of the few extant examples of early polyphony. [74] It was first performed in 1551 during
a pageant at Rouen honoring King Henry II of France and Queen
Catherine de 'Medici. In the festive procession, it was sung by "the
worthy ladies sitting in the float of Religion."[75] The same composition was described by Drinker:

> When King Henry II of France travelled to Rouen,
> he too was entertained by a pageant. The chron-
> icle of the festival describes a slow chariot on
> which ladies representing Vesta, Royal Dignity,
> Triumphant Virtue, Respect, and Awe rode while
> they sang a song of praise to the king. The very
> words and music that they sang are still in ex-
> istence--a four part motet for three soprano
> voices and one alto by H. Lecouteux. [76]

This procession was also the subject of a painting by Cassoni, which
further documents not only the event, but the female choir performance.

IV. Castrati Singers

During the sixteenth century and for a considerable period afterwards castrati singers gained increased prominence. There are conflicting statements regarding their origin. Bowman, for example,
made the following observation:

> The origin of the castrato voice seems to be
> entirely obscure, as only a few facts can be
> found regarding it prior to its prevalence in
> Italian opera seria during the seventeenth and
> eighteenth centuries. ... We have no trustworthy
> information on whether castrati were used in
> the earliest church music. [77]

The practice may be centuries old. Lang had reasons for thinking that "the origin of castration for the sake of a musical career goes back to age-old Oriental practices."[78] The rise in importance of castrati singers at this time must be attributed generally to the needs of both opera and the church. According to Bowman:

> There were many reasons why the castrato ap-
> — peared on the scene and why he was able to
> reach such heights of glory and fame. Probably
> one of the most important sociological reasons
> was the exclusion of women from the choirs of
> the Roman Church. Boys' voices could be sub-
> stituted for women's voices, as now, but there
> was one serious drawback--their voices were
> very short-lived.[79]

Although castration for musical purposes was a controversial moral issue, castrates were extensively employed in nearly all of Europe except France, where the practice was considered an affront against nature. Bowman wrote:

> Even in puritan England, the artificial male
> soprano held the center of the stage for nearly
> two centuries. The castrati were masters over
> their vocal organs and possessed power unat-
> tainable by women.[80]

Although the church had been neither the leader nor initiator in the development of female singing, but rather the follower of secular trends, this pattern may have been reversed in the use of castrates. Bukofzer stated that:

> The beginnings of the castrato practice were
> intimately connected with the Papal chapel in
> Rome where castrati appeared for the first
> time as early as 1562.[81]

Lang also gave the date of 1562 for the first entrance of castrati into the papal choir.[82] As might be expected, the influence of Rome quickly spread. Grout has written that "by the end of the seventeenth century, [castrati] were a usual feature in Italian churches in spite of periodic pronouncements by the Popes against the custom."[83]

Concerning papal condemnation of the practice of castration, there are conflicting statements. "By 1625," wrote Bowman, "the contraltini were superseded by the castrati and Pope Clement VIII declared officially that castrati for church choirs was 'Ad honorem

Dei'"[84] Lang, however, insisted that the practice of castration was never approved by the church, merely tolerated. [85]

By the late 1700's the incongruous nature of the practice was being condemned, for as Bowman related:

> The death penalty was provided for those who per-
> formed the operation and excommunication to every-
> one concerned in it--unless done (as often pretend-
> ed) on account of some disorder and with the con-
> sent of the boy. [86]

Whatever the nature of the official position, castrati were employed in the Sistine Choir from the middle of the sixteenth century
up to the nineteenth century, a long period of tacit church endorsement. The practice actually continued even longer, until Pope Leo
XIII (1878-1903) formally ended the practice in Italy of castration
for purposes of singing. [87]

The early writers of opera in the seventeenth century were
quick to employ the castrati, but it must be pointed out that castrati
were employed outside the church prior to the birth of the new art
form. Biehl wrote:

> According to Michael Praetorius' report, the
> Munich Court (1560) had under Orlando di Las-
> so thirteen contraltos, fifteen tenors, and twelve
> basses, and along with them sixteen choirboys
> and five or six eunuchs. The latter make the
> small number of boys possible for each replaced
> two or three boys. [88]

Several sources list Monteverdi's <u>Orfeo</u> in 1607 as the first
opera in which castrati appeared. An earlier opera, <u>Euridice</u> by
Peri (1600), employed a natural soprano, Vittoria Archilei, and
other accounts show that even in this newly rising field of musical
endeavor, women were not altogether excluded. According to Bowman:

> There are not sufficient full records of the casts
> of early operas to enable us to trace fully the
> change from normal voice distribution when the
> musical drama began, to the abnormality of the
> casting of the male soprano in the leading role.
> The few existing examples from intermezzi and
> musical dramas of the sixteenth century show
> that the composers of that era treated the voices
> naturally. [89]

Even so, opera was soon dominated by the use of castrati.

In addition to Monteverdi, other leading composers who wrote

for castrati singers included Cavalli, Cesti, Pergolesi, Scarlatti,
Hasse, Handel, Gluck and Mozart. [90] There were many advantages
to the castrato voice, some of which were detailed by Bowman:

> The singing apparatus of a castrato combined the
> larynx of a youth (emasculation prevents muscular
> change in this organ) with the chest and lungs of
> an adult. It therefore combined an unusually wide
> range with a sound of great power and of a special
> timbre which exercised great fascination upon the
> audience. [91]

Castrati could continue their careers for a long time; in some
cases their quality, in Grout's words, "often remained unimpaired
after as many as forty years of singing. "[92]

The advent of castrati singing in opera resulted in a number
of curious phenomena. Their popularity and their appeal caused the
lower male voices to disappear almost entirely from early opera
seria. [93] In addition to this, or perhaps as a result, castrates were
assigned the feminine roles. That early opera audiences tolerated
the seeming incongruity of male castrati taking female parts testifies
to the fact that the audiences were mostly interested in vocal virtu-
osity, in which the castrati singers were supreme. The accurateness
with which those roles were portrayed was not to be of major concern for some time.

The reign of the male soprano was in its glory in the days of
Handel, and Italian opera still employed the artificial voice during
the early years of Mozart's career. The role of "Siface" in Mozart's
Mitridate as performed in Milan in 1770 was taken by a male soprano. [94] While castrati were used in the church well into the eighteenth century, in opera the practice soon waned. In Venice, as
early as 1680, according to the French traveler Limojon de St.
Didier, female singers were not only used, but were highly regarded. St. Didier wrote of the Venetian opera: "They commonly have
the best Women Singers of all Italy...."[95] Harman and Milner mentioned at least three outstanding women opera singers during the so-
called "golden age of castrati". Referred to as cantarices (i.e. virtuoso women singers), they were Francesca Guzzoni (1700-1770),
Faustina Bordoni (1693-1781), the wife of Hasse, and Vittoria Tesi
(1700-1775). Despite his predilection for using castrati, even Handel

ceased to write for these singers after his oratorio <u>Deborah</u>.[96]

Gradually the art of the castrati declined, even in Italy. Perhaps this was due in part to a growing realization that the practice
was monstrous. According to Lang,

> There was, however, another weighty reason for
> the return to a variety of voices ranging from
> bass to soprano and sung by persons of correspond-
> ing character, and that was the ever-increasing
> popularity of the opera buffa with its flesh-and-
> blood figures. [97]

As elements of realism came into Italian opera plots, male
sopranos and contraltos were excluded. In Bowman's words:

> When dramatic verity claimed recognition on the
> stage the incongruous use of high voices had to be
> displaced by a normal distribution in which mascu-
> line and feminine qualities were appropriately dis-
> played. [98]

The last important composer to write castrato roles was Ros-
sini (1792-1868),[99] and with him ended a practice which lasted almost three hundred years. Women had once again survived an attempt to deprive them of responsible and natural participation in vocal performance.

V. The Baroque Era

Women continued their small role in public performance during
the Baroque period in music. Despite the threat of the castrati, they
not only became more active in music but gained increased public
acceptance. In ballet, for instance, where at first only men performed, a woman ballerina appeared on the public stage as early as 1681
in Lully's <u>Le Triumphe de L'Amour</u>. [100] A woman appeared on the
English public stage in a performance of <u>Siege of Rhodes</u> as early
as 1656, an exceptionally early date for conservative England. [101]

The increased use of women in these and similar roles led to
establishment of schools to train women performers. As described
by Drinker:

> The demand for trained singers to take part in
> operas and oratorios prompted musicians to found
> special schools for the instruction of music. Hence,
> one of the new movements of the seventeenth and
> eighteenth centuries was the institution of schools
> for girls.... One of the first schools for the pro-
> fessional woman performer was founded in France

by Lully.... In Hamburg, a municipal theater
was established... and later, almost every city
in Europe, England and the Americas had several conservatories of music which... expected
the attendance of girls.... [102]

Out of the demand of such schools for suitable literature came a
number of worthwhile compositions expressly scored for treble voices.
Most notable among them are <u>Dido</u> <u>and</u> <u>Aeneas</u> by Purcell, written
in 1689 for a boarding school for girls, and the <u>Miserere</u> of Hasse,
written in 1728 for the girl's chorus at the Conservatio dege' Incurabili. According to Drinker, Hasse also wrote a "charming litany
for the Empress Maria Theresa Vienna and her eight daughters to
sing in their private chapel."[103] And Charpentier wrote his famous
Christmas cantata for the young women at Port-Royal in the late
seventeenth century.

These conservatories, many of them for orphan girls, were a
milestone in the history of women in vocal music. Because of them
a literature for women's voices arose, and much of the previous
prejudice against women's choirs was overcome.

Performance of sacred music by nuns continued. The convents
of St. Agnes and St. Christina had established quite a rivalry in the
performance of liturgical song by the end of the seventeenth century,
and according to Drinker, "the famous walk to Longchamps [Paris]
originated in the eighteenth century as a pilgrimage of enthusiasts
who went to hear the nuns sing the <u>Tenebrae</u> on Good Friday."[104]

To be sure, the Church opposed the appearance of women on
the public stage and issued several decrees forbidding it. The decree
of Pope Innocent XI, in 1676, was meant to prohibit this in the
whole of Christendom, but it was not very successful either in secular or religious performances, as attested by the enthusiastic public response given to sacred music performed by the nuns. Para-
doxically, as Ritter observed:

> ... though the church forbade women, through-
> out medieval times, and by actual prohibition
> in the sixteenth century, to take any active mus-
> ical part in its services..., a feminine saint was
> adopted as patroness of music, and especially of
> church music... St. Cecilia. [105]

To the list of significant female singers in various ages must be added the names of Bach's second wife, Anna Magdalena Wülken, who was a Cöthen court singer, and Aloysia Weber, the sister of Mozart's wife. Both of these women established fair reputations as singers.

Few if any mixed choirs existed before the eighteenth century. Drinker, however, did list one such group as early as 1680--in France, [106] as might be expected, since that country never tolerated castrati. By the mid-eighteenth century, mixed choruses became somewhat more common, although as in the early hymn and psalm singing of this same general period, women usually sang only the soprano part. Said Drinker:

> In the first mixed choruses organized for sing-
> ing oratorios, women sang only the soprano parts.
> Often, in public performances, they merely rein-
> forced the choirboys' voices. In 1784 at the Handel
> commemoration in Westminster Abbey, for instance,
> eight ladies were permitted to assist the boys.
> . . . .
> The Stoughton Musical Society in America, organ-
> ized in 1774, gave women the treble, but not the
> alto parts. Only gradually did the women take a
> natural place among the singers. [107]

It was not until nearly a century later that Mendelssohn and Spohr first assigned alto parts to women in a mixed chorus. [108]

VI. Complete Liberation

By the time that the Romantic movement was firmly establish-ed, after about 1840, small mixed choruses became common. Wo-men were accepted members of such groups and the artificiality of male sopranos and contraltos in the performance of the new roman-tic songs and operas was no longer tolerated. By the middle of the nineteenth century, female participation in a fairly large number of secular choruses had successfully swayed public opinion concerning their acceptance into regular church choirs. Even in the Catholic church, women eventually were admitted to the religious choir--but not to a strictly liturgical choir--provided they sat in galleries at the back of the church. However, women were not, and are still not, admitted to membership in a wholly liturgical choir, be it Cath-olic or Protestant. Drinker distinguished between liturgical and non-liturgical choruses:

... Where church music is regarded as a kind of
sacred concert... women are admitted to the
choirs. But where music is a liturgy and the members of the liturgical choir are thought of as at-
tendants of the priest at the altar, women are excluded.... This prohibition applies whereever there
is liturgy in its ancient and traditional sense, in
the church service--whether the church be Catholic,
Greek Orthodox, Jewish or Protestant. [109]

Despite the general acceptance of women into mixed choruses,
both secular and religious, the nineteenth century did not produce
many outstanding women's choruses. Women's colleges gradually permitted amateur choral singing, and similar institutions associated
with the church also served as centers where women and/or girls
could function collectively as amateur singers. But suitable music
was not much more readily available than it had been in the past.
In fact, most of the choral literature written for women's voices
in the nineteenth century is traceable in many instances to the directors of such choruses; it was often composed by those men who
were trying to find music for their group to perform. Schubert, for
example, composed some music for Nanette Fröhlick's pupils, and
Brahms' famous Hamburg Frauenchör began from a simple request
of one of his pupils to arrange some folk music for her and her two
sisters to sing. The later significant contributions of Brahms to the
repertoire for women's choirs were a direct result of his inability
to find much suitable literature for the Frauenchör.

Women's choruses rarely performed on the public stage, even
through the end of the nineteenth century. It must be remembered
that the concerts given by Brahms and his young ladies were usually
private affairs. Even in the United States, where women had gained
numerous liberties, a public concert by a women's chorus in 1888
was not well received. [110]

The period following World War I saw a great acceleration in
the development and public acceptance of women's choruses. This
may have been partly due to the vastly increased number of girls'
schools and colleges as well as the rise of women's clubs. But it
must also be partly credited to Margaret Dessoff, who brought her
women's chorus from Frankfort to the United States in 1912 to participate in a great German Brahms Festival, in which she won

considerable public acclaim.

Largely due to the growth and improvement of collegiate groups, in recent years, the women's chorus is now recognized as a legitimate social and musical institution. As a result, there has been a considerable change for the better in both the quantity and quality of literature being composed for women's voices, especially by English, French and American composers.

---

1. Sophie Drinker Music and Women. New York, Coward-McCann, 1948. p. 63.

2. Ibid., p. 133.

3. Ibid., p. 71.

4. Albert A. Trever History of Ancient Civilization. New York, Harcourt, 1939. II: 595.

5. Drinker, loc. cit.

6. Ibid., p. 134.

7. Ibid., p. 137.

8. Ibid., p. 135.

9. Ibid., p. 160.

10. Ibid., p. 161.

11. Gustave Reese Music in the Middle Ages. New York, Norton, 1940. p. 63.

12. Drinker, op. cit., p. 160.

13. Reese, op. cit., p. 65.

14. Higini Angles "Gregorian Chant," New Oxford History of Music. New York, Oxford, 1954. II: 94.

15. Reese, op. cit., p. 68.

16. Jean Julian Dictionary of Hymnology. London, Murray, 1925. p. 206.

17. Arthur Elson Women's Work in Music. Boston, Page, 1903. p. 36.

18. Oliver Strunk (ed.) Source Readings in Music History. New York, Norton, 1950. p. 68.

19. Ibid.

20. Sophie Drinker Music and Women. New York, Coward-McCann, 1948. p. 68.

21. Paul H. Lang Music in Western Civilization. New York, W. W. Norton, 1941. p. 35.

22. Drinker, op. cit., p. 158.

23. Arthur Elson Women's Work in Music. Boston, L. C. Page, 1903. p. 37.

24. E. K. Chambers The Mediaeval Stage. Oxford, Clarendon Press, 1903. p. 235.

25. Drinker, op. cit., p. 179.

26. Jacques Handschin "Trope, Sequence and Conductus," New Oxford History of Music. New York, Oxford University Press, 1954. II: 139.

27. Drinker, op. cit., p. 190.

28. Ibid., p. 191.

29. Ibid., p. 190.

30. W. L. Smoldon "Liturgical Drama," New Oxford History of Music. New York, Oxford University Press, 1954. II: 219.

31. Ibid., p. 179.

32. Drinker, op. cit., p. 195.

33. Karl Young The Drama of the Medieval Church. New York, Oxford University Press, 1933. I: 13.

34. Ibid., p. 223.

35. Arthur Meese Choirs and Choral Music. New York, Charles Scribner's Sons, 1911. p. 64.

36. Drinker, op. cit., p. 208.

37. Gustave Reese Music in the Middle Ages. New York, Norton, 1940. p. 202.

38. Ibid., p. 205.

39. Fanny R. Ritter Woman as a Musician. New York, Edward Schuberth, 1876. p. 7.

40. Drinker, op. cit., p. 207.

41. Ibid., p. 213.

42. Frank Harrison "English Polyphony," New Oxford History of Music. New York, Oxford University Press, 1954. III: 372.

43. W. L. Smoldon "Liturgical Drama," New Oxford History of Music. New York, Oxford University Press, 1954. II: 188.

44. Gustave Reese Music in the Middle Ages. New York, W. W. Norton, 1940. p. 323.

45. The modern edition is volume LXV of the Henry Bradshaw Society, published in 1927.

46. Caroling was an already established practice in the parish church and secular circles.

47. J. B. L. Tolhurst (ed.) The Ordinale and Customary of the Benedictine Nuns of Barking Abbey. London, Henry Bradshaw Society, 1927. LXV: 373.

48. Ibid., p. 378.

49. Stephanus Hilpisch History of Benedictine Nuns. Collegeville, Minnesota, St. John's Abbey Press, 1958. p. 35.

50. Ibid., p. 43.

51. Ibid., p. 55.

52. Willi Apel Harvard Dictionary of Music. Cambridge, Harvard University Press, 1960. p. 635.

53. Paul H. Lang Music in Western Civilization. New York, W. W. Norton, 1941. p. 301.

54. Sophie Drinker Music and Women. New York, Coward-McCann, 1948. p. 216.

55. Ibid., p. 223.

56. Otto Kinkeldey "Equal Voices in the Acapella Period," Essays on Music. Cambridge, Harvard College, 1957. p. 102.

57. Drinker, loc. cit.

58. Lang, op. cit., p. 302.

59. Drinker, op. cit., p. 224.

60. Hans David (ed.) The Art of Polyphonic Song. New York, G. Schirmer, 1940. p. 32.

61. Stephanus Hilpisch History of Benedictine Nuns. Collegeville, Minnesota, St. John's Abbey Press, 1958. p. 70.

62. Alec Harman and Anthony Milner Man and His Music. Fairlawn, N. J., Essential Books, 1959. II: 89.

63. Drinker, op. cit., p. 267.

64. Harman and Milner, op. cit., p. 91.

65. Paul H. Lang Music in Western Civilization. New York, W. W. Norton, 1941. p. 302.

66. Gustave Reese Music in the Renaissance. New York, W. W. Norton, 1940. p. 316.

67. Lang, op. cit., p. 301.

68. Reese, op. cit., p. 409.

69. Harman and Milner, op. cit., p. 3.

70. Reese, op. cit., p. 656.

71. Drinker, op. cit., p. 218.

72. Arthur Elson Women's Work in Music. Boston, L. C. Page, 1903. p. 65.

73. Ibid., p. 66.

74. Hans David (ed.) The Art of Polyphonic Song. New York, G. Schirmer, 1940. p. 34.

75. Ibid.

76. Drinker, op. cit., p. 224.
77. Horace B. Bowman "The Castrati Singers and Their Music," (un-
     published Ph. D. dissertation, The University of Indiana), Blooming-
     ton, 1951. p. 24.
78. Lang, op. cit., p. 302.
79. Bowman, op. cit. p. 14.
80. Ibid., p. 22
81. Manfred Bukofzer Music in the Baroque Era. New York, W. W.
     Norton, 1947, 1947. p. 399.
82. Lang, loc. cit.
83. Donald J. Grout A Short History of Opera. New York, Columbia
     University Press, 1947. p. 196.
84. Bowman, op. cit., p. 29.
85. Lang, op. cit., p. 354
86. Bowman, op. cit., p. 75.
87. Ibid, p. 124.
88. Herbert Biehl Die Stimmkunst. Leipzig, Kistner and Siegel, 1931.
     p. 21.
89. Bowman, op. cit., p. 31.
90. Ibid., p. 91.
91. Ibid., p. 82.
92. Grout, op. cit., p. 196.
93. Bowman, op. cit., p. 20.
94. Ibid., p. 33.
95. Grout, op. cit., p. 103.
96. Alec Harman and Anthony Milner Man and His Music. Fairlawn,
     N. J., Essential Books, 1959. p. 279.
97. Paul H. Lang Music in Western Civilization. New York, W. W.
     Norton, 1941. p. 449.
98. Bowman, op. cit., p. 123.
99. Grout, op. cit., p. 339.
100. Harman and Milner, op. cit., II:171.
101. Ibid., p. 184.
102. Sophie Drinker Music and Women. New York, Coward-McCann,
      1948. p. 236.
103. Ibid., p. 225.
104. Ibid., p. 224.
105. Fanny R. Ritter Woman as a Musician. New York, Edward Schu-
      berth, 1876. p. 8.
106. Drinker, op. cit., p. 248.
107. Ibid.
108. Ibid.
109. Ibid., p. 249.
110. Ibid., p. 256.

Chapter III
Criteria Used for Selection

Selection of music for inclusion in this study is based on a number of criteria. Investigations in the related field of esthetics were the most helpful. Second in importance were the written opinions of recognized composers, performers and music critics. Third, the writer used his own observations of those elements which comprise a musical composition of high artistic merit. These observations, carefully analyzed, are based on a number of years of experience in conducting music scored for women's vocal combinations.

A fourth method for establishing valid criteria was that of submitting a preliminary list of criteria to a jury of recognized choral experts for their endorsement, amendment or suggestions as to validity. Such a method was used in a 1948 study by Christy but it revealed no significant differences between his own criteria and those arrived at by his jury of experts. Christy made two pertinent observations regarding his study. He concluded that "obtaining additional responses from similar judges could not be expected to change the results materially."[1] Secondly, he stated:

> It should be pointed out that the jury in this instance did not consist of a few random samplings from a much larger available group of similar character. It is considered improbable, if not impossible, to obtain another group of one hundred equally experienced and nationally recognized authorities in the United States. Since the possibility for further sampling of a similar nature appears to be well-nigh exhausted, it may be assumed that an adequate sampling of expert opinion was obtained and that the data thus secured approximate closely the data which would be obtained if the opinion of all possible judges of similar experience and standing were canvassed. [2]

For these reasons, the jury approach to forming criteria has not been used in the present study.

Selection of works for this list was made on the basis of what

can be called an evaluative criticism, derived from an understanding
of music esthetics, a term which applies more to the quality of a
work than to its technical aspects. While some of the criteria employed are of a scientific or technical analytical nature, the criteria
refer in general to the quality of the music and to its esthetic nature. While it may be highly desirable to establish a valid scientific
measure of determining merit, worth or beauty, no such means has
yet been devised. Scientific methods, such as the jury employed by
Christy, can give a consensus on what works of art contain elements
of merit and beauty, but cannot produce value judgments. Regarding
this problem, Bernstein asked:

> Can anyone explain in mere prose the wonder of
> one note following or coinciding with another so
> that we feel that it is exactly how those notes
> had to be? Of course not. No matter what ra-
> tionalists we may profess to be, we are stopped
> cold at the border of this mystic area. [3]

Studies in the field of esthetics or of evaluation of arts, such as
those by Vernon, Burkhoff and others, generally set up more or less
arbitrary examples of the expressive and the beautiful. However,
Langer noted that:

> Works of art are not usually comparable. Only
> prize juries have to evaluate them with refer-
> ence to some standard, which is inevitably arbi-
> trary, and in many cases inapplicable. A com-
> petent jury does not even define a standard. If
> it consists of people who have developed their
> powers of perception with long conversance with
> the order of art (i.e. poetry, sculpture, music,
> etc.) in which their judgements are to be made,
> intuition will guide the verdict. [4]

Most studies dealing with attempts to measure appreciation in the
arts emphasize the impossibility of obtaining an accurate standard
for art evaluation. There is no general agreement on the meaning
of such terms as "value", "merit", "good", nor even for the expression "work of art". Unsatisfactory as it may seem to some
readers, it must be concluded that these are terms which, though
undefinable, nevertheless carry with them a mutual empathic con-
notation among artists within a common discipline.

I. Intuitionalists and Rationalists

In analyzing a work of art, there exist at least two opposing schools of thought: the intuitionalists, who believe that beauty is self-evident and therefore cannot be analyzed, and the rationalists, who contend that things are beautiful because of formal structure which may be scientifically analyzed. Among those intuitionalists who maintain that the arts are incomprehensible by logic and therefore closed to scientific investigation is Max Schoen. Schoen defined the function of esthetics as follows:

> Aesthetics does not pretend to give a definition of an object of beauty, which would imply that any object that would comply with the specifications of the definition would be beautiful to any person coming in contact with it. [5]

Schoen's position may be described as the individualistic attitude to esthetics, for he maintained that the perception of beauty is a highly individual experience.

Rationalists, on the other hand, contend that since universality of approval or the "test of time" is what determines greatness, the value of a work of art is not individual, but social. Lalo seems to support this position; indeed, most writers who contend that art is created for an audience or that the essence of an art work depends unequivocally on shared experience with an audience would also uphold the social point of view.

The two opposing theories are described by Parker:

> Some thinkers have believed that there exist principles which can be applied to works of art to test their beauty with a certainty equal to that of the principles of logic in their application to inferences.... These principles, they would admit, are more difficult of application than the simpler logical rules, owing to the greater subtlety and complexity of art, yet, when found, have an equal validity within their own field. On the other hand, the view that there is no disputing about taste has never lacked adherents. According to this view, criticism can only be a report of personal, enthusiastic appreciation or repugnance without claim to universality. [6]

Both positions have much to recommend them, and in all probability both represent a degree of truth.

Yet, while most art works are conceived with an audience in mind, thus lending themselves to the social theory, art is capable of communicating to an audience only to the extent that the audience is responsive or is capable of being reached. Thus the work of art can be perceived only individually. Langer attested to this when she stated: "All knowledge goes back to experience; we cannot know anything that bears no relation to our experience."[7] In his "experiential" philosophy, Dewey gave emphatic support to this position. He said:

> To perceive, a beholder [or listener] must create his own experience... comparable to those the original producer underwent. The one who is too lazy, idle, or underrated in convention to perform this work will not see or hear. His 'appreciation' will be a mixture of scraps of learning with conformity to norms of conventional admiration and with a confused, even if genuine, emotional excitation. [8]

For many, the individual perception of a work of art will be the individual emotional experience derived from it and may be the only measure by which they may judge the art work. But such a position contains many inherent weaknesses, not the least of which is a lack of agreement on emotional meaning and significance. As Dewey argues, such a position leaves no provision for the education and cultivation of taste. Therefore emotional reaction is not a valid criterion for judging a work of art. [9]

II. Isolationism, Contextualism and Relativism

Fortunately, the issue of value standards has received considerable attention and a number of tenable theories have been put forth in recent years. Isolationism generally suggests the position of "art for art's sake" and may be thought of as the philosophical theory of the "discovered good". Schwadron suggests that in this theory the "structural insight remains the paramount criterion for standards of the ultimate good."[10] In other words, the significance of music is tonal, not extra-musical. It is not meaningful because it is descriptive or expressive of something. This position differs from the intuitionalist point of view in that the intuitionalists attach little importance to scientific or structural analysis. It is important to note,

however, that the structural insight referred to in the isolationist
point of view is acknowledged only in objective terms, not in subjective evaluations of structure.

Contextualism suggests the position of "art for man's sake" and
may be thought of as the general philosophical level of the "received
good". The philosophical theory of contextualism is generally based
on a traditional reactionary level, essentially social realism. According to Schwadron, contextualism "stresses the spiritual context
of music as expressive of life experiences"[11] and depends upon widespread social acceptance. The masses, not the experts, should judge
artistic work. This position does not differ markedly from the ra-
tionalist point of view.

The third philosophical theory is that of relativism, which is
a combination of the above two views. It recognizes the desire for
improvement which can be brought about by education. It acknow-
ledges the need for cultivating taste, yet admits to a plurality of
tastes, and it confesses to the need for a system of critical standards, while permitting values to be culturally determined and of a
relative nature. [12] Relativism permits esthetic criteria to be flexible
and to undergo periodic re-evaluation. As Schwadron has indicated:
a work of art should be evaluated according to the established or
accepted criteria of the time in which it is being evaluated.

III. Points of Criteria

Faced with these differing viewpoints, the reader might justifi-
ably ask, "Which theory has the most validity in judging musical
worth?" Certainly, there can be no arbitrary disavowal of such influences as emotional appeal, experiential affinity and expressive content. These are all important considerations in evaluating a given
selection, perhaps not in a scientific or syntactical analysis, but
certainly in terms of obtaining the desired audience response to programing. Though it would be foolhardy to forbid their inclusion in
establishing selective criteria, their role will be relegated to one
of secondary importance in criteria to be established. Of first importance will be a leaning on isolationist theory, which emphasizes
objective aspects of a musical selection, for herein lie more defensible and valid considerations.

Criteria established in the present study are as follows:

1. A high degree of merit as a work of art; that
   is, inherent esthetic beauty in a piece of music.

2. A text of literary value

3. Technical components well conceived.

   a. Elements of melody, harmony, rhythm
      and texture are interesting.

   b. Musical and textual phrases and sections
      are sensitively constructed and treated.

   c. Accompaniment, when employed, enhances
      the work.

   d. Demands on performers with regard to
      tessitura and acceptable vocal limitations
      (intervals and phrase lengths) are reason-
      able.

4. Probable appeal to both listener and performer.

A High Degree of Merit

There exist three areas of musical response and enjoyment: the
sensuous, in which tonal combinations provide pleasures of sound;
the associative, which induces thought connections to other ideas;
and the syntactical, whereby the mind is stimulated by orderly tonal
arrangements and relationships. All three of these areas are important, and most music involves all three, though usually giving
emphasis to only one. But which is of more value? The position
taken here is that the syntactical elements are the more important.
Reimer supports this choice when he states:

> ... while we might evaluate the response of
> listeners on the basis of weighing sensuous-
> associative and syntactical elements present in
> the response, we can only evaluate musical
> works syntactically. For the degree of presence
> or absence of sensuous and associative aspects
> in a piece of music is a completely subjective
> matter. Who is to say which piece has greater
> sensuous appeal or evokes the more poignant
> associations?[13]

Although subjective analysis or response must receive some consideration in determining this first criterion, the syntactical or objective aspect must receive primary importance.

Reimer outlines several interesting points pertaining to an

objective or syntactical analysis of a musical selection. He states
that most persons recognize certain technical criteria for excellence
in a musical work, such as consistency of style, clarity of basic
intent, variety, and unity. But Reimer is quick to point out that
these technical criteria may be found in many pieces of music which
can hardly be labeled as "great", and that therefore their presence
alone is not sufficient to differentiate real quality.

Essentially, a piece of music which has musical worth is one
which possesses the important qualities of art: richness of imagina-
tion and invention, and intensity and lucidity of expression. Such in-
tangible elements as expression, beauty, and human significance
must also be considered. "A successful musical composition,"
writes Weinstock, "like every good work in any art...expresses
pre-existing meanings and by so doing creates meanings that could
not have existed before."[14] The work of art must communicate
meaningfully, must "reach" or "get to" the listener in some manner. This perhaps explains why so many of the newer composition
techniques, such as serial form, atonality, polytonality and others,
are thus far relatively unaccepted other than from the standpoint of
their intellectual aspects.

Within these newer forms and indeed, as far as their techniques
are understood by the general public, there is little of a common
bond of experience or emotional significance. Likewise, among many
lesser composers and arrangers who continually flood the commer-
cial market of choral music with "popular" and "novelty" selections,
the presence of emotional elements in their efforts can hardly be dis-
cerned. On this topic, Thomson has said, "What makes possible
the writing of good music, beyond that talent for handling sound that
is required for being a musician at all, is emotional sincerity and
intellectual honesty."[15] It would seem that the great composers of
all ages have had both qualities in abundance.

The second part of Weinstock's statement, that a true work of
art is capable of creating meanings that could never have existed
before, is equally significant, and not unlike Langer's observation:
"Just as words can describe events we have not witnessed, places
and things we have not seen, so music can present emotions and

moods we have not felt, passions we did not know before. "[16] Lending credence to this comment is the remark of a friend, who in discussing his first hearing of the Bach Violin Concerto in E major, attempted to describe a rare musical experience. "After the slow movement," he said, "there was an incredibly long interval of absolute silence; of that dumbfounded silence in which men contemplate a revelation." Such is the power of a truly great work of art.

There are probably several valid ways to determine merit in a work of art. A number of writers have suggested that there are three facets of a work toward which a competent criticism of art must direct attention: first, the essential content of the work, its subject; second, the treatment of that subject, its form; and third, the human significance of the whole. Goethe shaped the same three questions thus:

> 1. What has the artist tried to do?
> 2. How has he done it?
> 3. Was it worth doing?[17]

Siegneur de Franeuse in the early eighteenth century considered this matter in a cleverly written dialogue between himself and an imaginary countess. In slightly condensed form his remarks are as follows:

> There are two great ways of knowing good and
> bad things; by our inward feeling and by the
> rules. . . . The authority of the rules is consider-
> able, but after all it is not a law. Inward feel-
> ing is still less sure, because each should dis-
> trust his own. . . . I think that in this uncertainty
> and confusion the remedy is to lend to the in-
> ward feeling the support of the rules. . . and
> therefore I am persuaded that good taste is the
> most natural feeling, corrected or confirmed
> by the best rules. [18]

The rules to which he refers are rather simply stated:

> A piece of music should be natural, expressive,
> and harmonious. . . . These are the three great
> important rules which one must apply to the airs
> [music] that the inward feeling has approved. . . . A
> last rule, which must be added. . . is always to
> abhor excess.[19]

In the selection of music, at least two temptations often beset the conscientious choral director. First, he may be tempted to judge

a piece of music solely on the basis of its composer, the assump-
tion being that if the composer is one who is held in high regard,
then the music must also be of high merit. As Quantz indicates,
eighteenth-century musicians and critics were conscious of the
dangers of such preconceived notions:

> ... we are usually inclined to begin by asking
> who the composer is in order to be guided by
> this in [forming] our judgment. Does the piece
> prove to be by someone to whom we have con-
> ceded our approval in advance, it is at once
> unhesitatingly pronounced beautiful. Does the
> contrary apply, or have we some objection to
> the author's person, the whole piece passes
> for worthless. [20]

That many works by composers of recognized (and revered) status
are conspicuously absent from the recommended list in this study
(see Chapter Four) should not be misunderstood as constituting
merely careless omissions.

The second temptation is that of programing music because of
its historical significance. On this point, Tovey states: "... the
historical position of a work of art is not a matter of aesthetic importance. A work of art normally exists for its own sake and not
for its position in history."[21] Various historical styles or periods
may, of course, be represented on a program of choral music; but
a piece of music must be regarded not purely from a historical
point of view, but from an artistic one.

Of all the criteria one can use in selecting music, none is more
important than this first one.

Any piece of choral music that commands serious attention from
a conductor should be a work of art. Only when such a standard is
clearly evident is the selection worthy of the time and energies of
both performers and audience.

Text Which Has Literary Value

In judging music, the second and third criteria, literary value
of the text and technical components, really cannot be considered
apart from the general category of worth, for they are part and
parcel of what constitutes worth. Even so, as important aspects of
the total picture, they deserve at least passing attention.

There is danger that choral conductors may be misled into judging the merit of the text on the basis of its source. This situation
is much akin to the temptation pointed out by Quantz of considering
musical worth on the sole basis of the established eminence of the
composer. Merely because a text by a man of recognized talent has
been set to music is little reason to suppose that the end result is
necessarily successful. It should also be kept in mind that the literature of choral music abounds with examples of hackneyed and completely unmusical settings of Bible verse, a text source of generally
undisputed quality.

While the literary value of many texts may be spoiled by a poor
musical treatment, much choral literature has enhanced a mediocre
text by sensitive musical treatment. Langer has significantly observed:

> The measure of a good text, a good libretto,
> even a good subject for music, is simply its
> transformability into music; and that depends
> on the composer's imagination. Thus Mozart,
> working on The Seduction from the Serail,
> wrote to his father, who had found all sorts
> of fault with the libretto: "As for Stephanie's
> work, you are quite right, of course.... I
> know well enough that his versification is not
> of the best, but it falls in so well with my
> musical ideas... that I can't help liking it,
> and I am ready to bet that in the perform-
> ance of the work you won't notice any short-
> comings. "[22]

Langer continues: "When a composer puts a poem to music, he an-
nihilates the poem and makes a song. "[23] That is why trivial or
sentimental lyrics may be as good texts as great poems. Beethoven
employed the greatest literature of his day, using Goethe, Schiller
and their contemporaries, but Schubert often used decidedly second-
rate material, such as that of Müller, in creating superb vocal music.

The degree of importance of text in choral music is one of curious dimensions. To the performers of the music, there is little
quarrel about its significance, for they are involved with meanings,
subtleties, shadings and expressiveness and they are obviously aware
of what the text says. Probably every choral conductor has experienced the frustration of working with a piece of music which fails

to "strike the mark" in either rehearsal or performance. More often than not, the mystery is solved when he makes a careful scrutiny of the text and its rejection by the singers. But the importance of the text to the audience is not as real as the conductor might suppose. The truth of the matter is that, "when words enter into music they are no longer prose or poetry, they are elements of the music.[24] Auden also shares this view: "In song, poetry is expendable, syllables are not. "[25] In The Pleasures of Music, Barzun reports on an experiment conducted by Vernon. Vernon discovered that a concert audience of average musical level took little notice of the text of a song performed. In a specific concert, sixty-three percent of the audience did not notice at all, and only six percent were definitely aware that the words sung to a song by Thomas Campion were nonsense. [26]

This is not to suggest that literary value of the text is of little consequence; it does illustrate that it is a factor of secondary importance in evaluating choral music. A good general rule when considering text as a criterion is Hirt's suggestion that the text should be "comprehensible and within the emotional experience of the singers, either actually or vicariously. "[27]

The judge of choral music should look for an expressive treatment of both literary and musical elements, if he wishes to produce an entirely new creation which will be not only compatible, but uniquely artistic.

Technical Components

As in the case of the preceding criterion, the degree to which technical components may be regarded as separate factors in judging music is open to some question. Although effective handling of technical details is important, it probably has little significance in the ultimate value of the piece. The mishandling of such details, on the other hand, can hardly produce a work of art. About literature, Barzun writes:

> It has long been recognized... that true criticism does not consist in the exclusive analysis of an author's grammar and syntax. A poem is not judged or explained by listing the metaphors, constructions and idioms which it employs. [28]

Likewise, a painting is judged not solely on the hues of its colors, the lines of perspective, or the brush technique employed, but rather on the overall effect it creates. As Mendl stated the case:

> However closely we may analyze a work of art or discuss its technical characteristics, we can never bridge the gulf between technique, skill, science on the one hand, and spirit, emotion, imagination on the other. [29]

Similarly, an artistic piece of music consists of more than interesting chord progression, skillful counterpoint or complicated rhythmic patterns. It must have meaningful relationships and expressive content, sensitively presented.

Technical components are important to the general effect achieved, but the value judgment extends far beyond them. In this regard Tovey drew the following conclusion:

> ... the duty of the artist is not to contribute to an edifice entitled Art with a capital A. There is no such edifice. There are [only] individual works of art, and it is the business of each individual work to be a whole. [30]

If its import to a work of art is so minimal, why is this criterion even listed? Performers are constantly challenged to meet the technical demands placed upon them by composers but the only elements which the listener is even likely to be cognizant of are those of melody, harmony, rhythm and texture, and even these to only a superficial extent. What is more likely to be the focal point of most listeners is the sheer ocean of pleasurable sound in which he enjoys bathing. To the musically tutored, however, great art is more than a direct sensuous pleasure.

The technical components of a given work do then constitute an important part of a work of art, increasingly so when a higher level of understanding and beauty is sought. They may not always be evaluated or considered as separate entities, but the literature of music contains many examples wherein they may be so considered. The use of a Russian air by Beethoven in one of his Rasoumovsky quartets and Moussorgsky's use of the same air in his music-drama Boris Godounoff clearly emphasize that the element of melody in both works is a component to be evaluated. Likewise, the accompaniment of the Bach-Gounod Ave Maria must be evaluated as a separate component, especially when it is recognized that it exists as a separate work under the title "C major Prelude" in Bach's Well Tempered Clavier: Book I. The material used and the manner in which it is handled may directly influence or determine the actual life of a musical work, as well as its worth. Thompson wrote:

> Much music has been important to its own time because of its manner or details of its workmanship, only to fall by the wayside thereafter because the material was not of the quality to command admiration after the manner was no longer the vogue and when advances of technique had made commonplace the once admired workmanship. Other music has lived on because of the power and beauty of the material, when manner and workmanship came to be recognized as outdated. [31]

Technical components, like the text, must be judged by the conductor as integral parts of the work under consideration. While they may be evaluated individually for performance purposes, they must ultimately give way to esthetic evaluation of the whole. They are important, apart from their influence upon the performers, only as they comprise and complement the vitality of the art work. Thus they deserve careful attention in any systematic evaluation of a musical selection.

Probable Appeal to Both Listener and Performer

Initially it was thought that this fourth criterion, probable appeal to both listener and performer, should have no influence on the music to be included in this bibliography, for fear that the quality of the music selected might thereby be lowered. Happily, however, the general public has become far more sophisticated in its musical taste and has demonstrated its eagerness to hear good music well performed. More and more audiences seem interested in being esthetically nurtured rather than merely entertained. Thousands of amateur singers who once demanded popular music as a basic part of their repertoire are now performing music of more substantial quality. Conductors have discovered the truth of the recent axiom of composer Bacon: "In matters of public taste, no less than with

the individual, it should be noted that just as liking something is
conducive to doing it well, so also is doing it well conducive to
liking it. "[32] Indeed, among choral groups and their audiences an
increase in the quality of the singing performance has often led to
an increase in the quality of the music being sung.

Better quality music has greater appeal to both listeners and
performers for the reason that great music is meaningful and significant to people. We may not be able to determine exactly what it
signifies--an ambiguity which is actually one of the assets of mus-
ic--but we know that it does convey meaning. Indeed, if it cannot
express meaning, in all likelihood neither does it appeal to people,
nor is it a work of art.

Certain composers have been accused from time to time of not
keeping in touch with the general public and of writing for some
cultural elite. Perhaps the obscurity of some composers may be
traced directly to this cause, but it is hardly true of the great
masters. Butler in writing of Bach remarks:

> It is imputed to him for righteousness that he
> goes over the heads of the general public and
> appeals mainly to musicians. But the greatest
> men do not go over the heads of the masses,
> they take them rather by the hand. [33]

Great composers are able to take the people by the hand precisely
because they too as human beings have a knowledge of human feelings, and these feelings are what they are attempting to express.
In writing of Monteverdi, Parry states:

> Monteverdi belonged to that strongly defined
> order of composers who are not so much im-
> pelled by the mere delight of music itself as
> by the opportunities it offers to interpret vivid-
> ly emotions, moods, human feelings, dramatic
> situations, pathetic incidents and exhilarating
> joys. They are the musicians who instinctively
> feel music's sphere in the scheme of things.
> ... they delve into human life and feeling, and
> get their highest inspirations from their keen
> sympathy with their fellow creatures and their
> insight into them. [34]

So it is, that these elements of expression are ever present in
a work of art, and it is likely to be those musical works which

contain such expressions which will have the greatest appeal to performer and listener.

1. Van A. Christy "Evaluation of Choral Music," Contributions
   to Education. New York, Bureau of Publications, Teachers
   College, Columbia University, 1948. p. 93.

2. Ibid., p. 21.

3. Leonard Bernstein "Speaking of Music," The Atlantic Monthly.
   December, 1957. p. 104.

4. Susanne K. Langer Feeling and Form. New York, Charles
   Scribner's Sons, 1953. p. 406.

5. Max Schoen Art and Beauty. New York, MacMillan, 1932. p. 13.

6. Dewitt Parker The Principles of Aesthetics. New York, Silver
   Burdet Co., 1920. pp. 127-128.

7. Susanne K. Langer Feeling and Form. New York, Charles
   Scribner's Sons, 1953. p. 390.

8. John Dewey Art as Experience. New York, Minton, Balch, 1934.
   p. 54.

9. John Dewey "Meaning of Value," Journal of Philosophy. Febru-
   ary, 1925. p. 131.

10. Abraham Schwadron "Interpretation of Philosophy and Aesthetics
    for Contemporary Music Education." (Unpublished Mus. A. D.
    dissertation, Boston University, 1962.) p. 176.

11. Ibid., p. 77.

12. Ibid., p. 93.

13. Bennett Reimer "Leonard Meyer's Theory of Value and Great-
    ness in Music," Journal of Research in Music Education. Wash-
    ington, Music Educators National Conference, Fall, 1962. X(2):92-
    93.

14. Herbert Weinstock Music as an Art. New York, Harcourt,
    Brace, 1953. p. 13.

15. Virgil Thomson The Art of Judging Music. New York, Alfred
    A. Knopf, 1948. p. 301.

16. Susanne K. Langer Philosophy in a New Key. Cambridge, Har-
    vard University Press, 1951. p. 222.

17. Marlies K. Danziger and W. Stacy Johnson An Introduction to
    Literary Criticism. Boston, D. C. Heath, 1961. p. 251.

18. Oliver Strunk (ed.) Source Readings in Music History. New York,
    W. W. Norton, 1950. p. 491.

19. Ibid., p. 493.

20. Ibid., p. 579.

21. Donald F. Tovey The Main Streams of Art and Other Essays.
    New York, Oxford University Press, 1949. p. 161.

22. Susanne K. Langer Feeling and Form. New York, Charles
    Scribner's Sons, 1953. p. 160.

23. Ibid. , p. 153.

24. Ibid. , p. 150.

25. W. H. Auden "Notes on Music and Opera," The Dyer's Hand
    and Other Essays. New York, Random House, 1962. p. 473.

26. Jacques Barzun The Pleasures of Music. New York, Viking
    Press, 1951. p. 187.

27. Charles C. Hirt Criteria for the Composing, Arranging and
    Editing of Choral Literature for the Senior High School Mixed
    Chorus. Los Angeles, Affiliated Musicians, 1954. p. 7.

28. Barzun, op. cit. , p. 10.

29. R. W. S. Mendl The Soul of Music. London, Rockliff, 1950. p.
    278.

30. Donald F. Tovey The Main Streams of Art and Other Essays.
    New York, Oxford University Press, 1949. p. 161.

31. Oscar Thompson Practical Musical Criticism. New York, M.
    Witmark and Sons, 1934. p. 57.

32. Ernst Bacon Words on Music. Syracuse, Syracuse University
    Press, 1960. p. 179.

33. Samuel Butler "Note Books," An Anthology of Music Criticism.
    compiled by Norman Demuth, London, Eyre and Spottiswoode,
    1947. p. 99.

34. (Sir) Hubert Parry "The Significance of Monteverdi," An An-
    thology of Music Criticism, compiled by Norman Demuth, London,
    Eyre and Spottiswoode, 1947. p. 21.

Chapter IV
Recommended Compositions for Women's Voices

The musical selections for women's voices which appear on the following pages have been subjected to the critical standards listed and described in the preceding chapter and have been found worthy of inclusion in this selected list.

I. Works Included

There has been no attempt to make this list all-inclusive, although a large number of compositions were examined with great care. The vast bulk of arrangements of works originally composed for other vocal combinations were not considered to be appropriate to this study. However, a significant number of excellent choral works, particularly from the Renaissance period, and pre-existing melodies such as folk songs and carols have been successfully arranged for women's voices. Some of these have been listed, though not annotated, if they met the high standard of the established criteria.

The list also includes a number of compositions which were originally scored for equal voices, but not necessarily for women's voices. Often, according to the practice at the time of their composition, composers assigned many of these works to either high voice or low voice combinations.

Occasionally it was difficult to determine the original status of a composition whose modern edition indicates that it has been adapted, edited or transcribed for women's voices. In some cases this might signify merely a transposition of pitch or, at the opposite extreme, it might mean that an original SATB work has been edited to include the essential harmonies and vocal lines, but is now rescored for women's voices. Since little reliability could be guaranteed in determining the extent of those adaptations, only a small number of such compositions have been included.

In addition to the musical works included in this list, all of

which are published separately, there are many excellent compositions which appear in collections. Those used are listed in the indices under the title of the collection.

Finally, there are many compositions originally scored for women's voices, which are intended almost exclusively for the Roman
Catholic church service. Although many of these compositions are of
acceptable musical quality, they have been omitted from this study
because of their specialized nature.

II. Format of Annotations

The entry of each annotation follows the format described below:

Composer (arranged alphabetically by last name)	Publisher and catalog number of edition examined

Title of Composition

Number of vocal parts (solo assignments in parenthesis)	Grade of difficulty	Approximate length of composition

Descriptive Annotation

Type of accompaniment (if any)	Vocal range (lowest alto note to highest soprano note)

Other available editions (if any)

Arrangements which are included in this list specify the following information only:

Composer (or arranger)	Publisher and catalog number

Title of Composition

Number of vocal parts (and indication of accompaniment)	Name of Arranger or Editor

The abbreviations used for identifying arrangers and editors and
the abbreviations used for identifying publishers, together with their
addresses, are keyed and listed in the Appendix.

The durations listed for each composition should be regarded as
approximations. Since ideas of tempo and interpretation vary, it was
not considered practical to time each selection.

Publications containing several compositions, either by the same composer or different composers, will have each title listed in the same annotation. In such cases, the descriptive annotation has been generalized to include analysis of the publication as a whole rather than each work.

III. Explanation of Assigned Grades of Difficulty

The compositions listed have been categorized as easy, medium or difficult. These levels of difficulty were determined by a formula containing nine items of rehearsal or performance problems: (1) range, (2) melodic character of individual vocal lines, (3) harmonic elements, (4) rhythmic complexities, (5) complexities of text, (6) key signatures and inherent tonal relationships, (7) tempo, (8) physical demands and (9) accompaniment. Each of these items was considered in designating the selection as easy, medium or difficult in its musical nature.

What may prove to be difficult for one choir may well be easy for another, depending upon the abilities, proficiencies and capabilities of the choral organization. This grading system was applied on the hypothetical standard of what might be termed an average choir.

It is not suggested that this average choir would be found at either a high school or college level. Some high schools will have a choir that far exceeds this arbitrary standard, while many colleges may never achieve it.

The Average Choir

The following characteristics have been used to define what may be assumed to be an average choir:

1. A few sight readers who quickly grasp new music, comprising at least ten percent of the membership. They are essential to help the group hear the music in its early rehearsal stages and they serve to lead the others to a more rapid grasp and understanding of the notes.

2. A high percentage of members who learn notes quickly even though they remain somewhat dependent on the sight readers. They must be alert and rapid learners, so that the choir can sing confidently at an early stage of rehearsals.

3. Some familiarity and previous experience in singing literature of a nature similar to

that included in this study. Members are thus
able to anticipate normal patterns of sequence,
phrase construction and harmony and to trans-
fer their knowledge to new works, permitting
them to learn works with greater expedition
and confidence.

4. Capabilities for hearing and listening to intervals, rhythmic patterns, harmony parts and accompaniment. Members who listen to their own
chorus section, to the accompaniment, to interval leaps and to the other vocal parts relate
their role to the music and significantly decrease
the number of learning and refining attempts
necessary.

5. Sufficient capability to handle reasonable ranges
with ease. Sopranos and altos should have sufficient strength within their sections so that there
is confident assurance that extreme fringes of
their respective ranges will maintain both strength
and quality.

6. Chorus sections which are strong and independent
enough to cope with their own musical assignment
while help is being given to other parts.

7. Sufficient confidence in the director, the various
chorus sections and individual singers. Such confidence is important in minimizing hesitancy of
entrances and in developing dynamic levels, blend-
ing efforts and chord tone members.

8. An accompanist who is technically capable and
has a strong rhythmic sense. The accompanist
should not attempt to be a solo performer, but
must be a constant aid to the director and the
singers in giving pitches, phrasing musically
and presenting unfaltering rhythmic unity.

9. Patience, enthusiasm for the literature and a
high esprit de corps.

No choir, of course, can rise above the technical capabilities
and musical sensitivity of its conductor. The old adage that there
are no bad choirs, only bad conductors is probably more true than
is generally admitted. The standard of the average choir can be
met or exceeded only to the extent of the conductor's musical en-
dowments.

Graded Levels of Difficulty

The graded levels of difficulty of the music included in this
study were interpreted as follows:

Easy

1. The range is undemanding, and highly contained in that it rarely exceeds a tenth.

2. The melodic movement of all voice parts is predominantly diatonic, with few leaps outside the chords, little if any chromaticism, and conventional melodic resolutions.

3. The harmony is confined largely to strong chords of a given key, such as tonic, dominant, subdominant and an occasional secondary dominant chord. If and when modulations occur, they are smooth and generally prepared by the accompaniment. Few if any chords contain any chromatic alteration, unless due to strong melodic type influences such as in contemporary music. Any counterpoint present is of the simple "counter-melody" type and is generally limited to two-part counterpoint.

4. Rhythm is fairly uncomplex and largely within the normal time meter accents. Few if any meter changes occur, unless a complete shift from duple to triple meter takes place. No compound meter signatures such as 5/4 and 7/8 are used. No syncopated rhythmic patterns or hemiola effects are used which would present rhythmic complexity. Dotted rhythms or similar patterns when utilized are not isolated changes in the established rhythmic flow, but used as basic patterns throughout much of the work.

5. The musical setting of the text is rather simple and metrically set to fit the basic pulse and the normal uncomplex subdivisions of the established meter. The text is understandable and within the "experience range" of the performers.

6. The normal diatonic pattern of regular tones and semi-tones of the established key is such that it presents no problem of recall.

7. Tempos are not too fast, permitting ease of note-reading and fitting of the text.

8. Little physical demand is made with regard to dynamic contrasts or phrase endurance.

9. The nature of the accompaniment tends to support the harmonies and rhythms of the vocal lines. When independent, the accompaniment still remains simple and complementary to the vocal lines.

Medium

1. The ranges employed often approach the normal
   limits which are considered safe for amateur
   singers. Usually, however, such notes are
   thoughtfully prepared by being well placed within the phrases and, in the case of high notes,
   well supported either by octave doublings or
   full chordal harmony by the lower voices. Passages which include notes in the higher and
   lower ranges do not dwell on these notes for
   any undue length of time.

2. Melodic movement of the vocal lines, including
   inner voices, remains predominantly diatonic,
   although leaps exceeding a third are common.
   Some chromaticism is normal, particularly
   within inner parts, as a result of more advanced harmonic progressions. There is more
   independence of parts, as a result of greater
   freedom from rigid homophonic writing.

3. Harmonic structure is more varied and non-
   diatonic progressions become common. Modulations are still relatively easy to manage, although enharmonic interchanges of notes are
   more apt to appear. Many of the harmonies
   employed still may be consonant, although some
   tendencies to linear writing result in more independence of resultant chord members. Not
   infrequently, dissonances occur, although they
   are usually resolved. Altered chords become
   more common.

4. Rhythmic freedom is increased and independence of part writing often results in varied
   and independent rhythmic treatment of the
   several vocal lines. Meter signatures are not
   so rigidly adhered to with regard to metrical
   accents, and such effects as simple hemiolas
   become normal. Meter changes may become
   more frequent, although they are normally
   the more common duple and triple types.
   Dotted rhythms, varied patterns and greater
   tendencies toward imitative writing often result in an unrigid approach to rhythmic matters, and the accompaniment often adds further independence to the rhythmic treatment.

5. There is more independence of vocal writing,
   especially in the use of imitative and contrapuntal techniques, which often results in textual complexities of a modest nature. Frequently, compositions of this grade level will have
   some polytextual sections.

6. Key signatures are usually not a limitation. Occasionally, some passages may temporarily modulate to other keys or new key signatures will be introduced as needed. Most of the part writing still remains related to the key signature of the moment, however.

7. Tempo limitations are not a consideration and occasional changes of tempo are rather common. It may be assumed that compositions with a more complex or independent treatment of text, and those compositions which involve more complex intervalic skips and relationships, are consciously tempered by the composer with a logical tempo which is in reason with any other complexities which may be present.

8. Dynamic contrasts or demands upon the singers may be more extended and general length of the work may be increased. Also, more refined vocal control may often be implied by works which contain more subtleties of nuance, phrase and shading.

9. Accompaniments very often may be considerably independent of the vocal lines and they may involve more precise and complex rhythmic alterations. It should be noted also that much more music of this grade level will be unaccompanied, thus increasing the responsibilities of the singers toward greater accuracy of rhythm, harmony and intonation.

Difficult

1. Range, with the possible exception of low alto notes, probably is of little concern to the composer. At least he does not consider it a limiting factor.

2. Melodic or linear movement of the individual vocal lines is generally freely treated. Chromaticism is often present. Difficult interval skips such as those of the diminished, augmented, sevenths, and minor sixths are quite common, particularly as a result of the modern contrapuntal style and advanced harmonic progressions which are often employed. Normal melodic resolutions may often be entirely ignored, resulting in angular lines. Frequent parallel movement of fourths and fifths often results in non-diatonic lines, particularly within inner voices. Many of the Renaissance works are highly complex in their emphasis on counterpoint and imitation.

3. There is a tendency toward great harmonic
   freedom. Such devices as parallel movement,
   altered chords, deliberate dissonances and an
   increased amount of polyphony or counterpoint
   all contribute problems of hearing, intonation,
   independence of chorus sections and general
   vocal security. Polychordal or polytonal writing may create two simultaneous tonal centers,
   a problem which often is caused or complicated further by harmonically independent or advanced accompaniments.

4. Rhythmic variations often become highly complex, stressing negation of the bar lines
   which amateur singers depend upon so heavily.
   Hemiola effects as well as rapid and frequent
   changes of meter signature, including the more
   compound types, may occur. Complex and syncopated rhythmic motives and patterns are used
   more frequently and are often compounded by
   contrasting rhythms in some accompaniments
   or by varying and contrasting rhythms within
   the vocal parts.

5. Texts are often more complex in their basic
   literary meanings and polytextual effects appear as a natural result of imitation, counterpoint, and rhythmic variations. An increased
   number of texts set in Latin, German, French
   and Italian may be expected. Frequent meter
   changes, hemiolas and faster tempos may also
   increase textual problems.

6. The use of multiple tonalities, frequent modulations, semi-nontonal effects and increased
   chromaticism may contribute to added complexities with regard to key relationships.

7. Generally, tempo limitations are not in evidence and frequent changes of tempo are
   quite common.

8. There are often great physical demands placed
   upon singers and accompanist with regard to
   range, endurance and dynamic shadings, including sudden or frequent contrasts of power
   versus pianissimo passages.

9. Accompaniment parts range from virtuoso-
   type demands to extremes of simple, sensitive artistic tenderness, sometimes highly independent, yet often necessarily supportive of
   the vocal lines.

IV. Original Works

Abt, Franz　　　　　　　　　　　　　　　　　　　GS 5992

"Night"

SSA　　　　　　　　　Easy　　　　　　　　2 min.

Franz Abt composed chiefly songs (lieder) and part music for men's voices, although he also wrote a few works for female voices, such as this. The work is scored in a predominantly homophonic style, although the middle section is given over to part writing which is independently linear. The chief strength of this work is its lyrical melody, to which the other parts are fittingly subservient. The accompaniment tends to get a little monotonous in its constant reiteration of a broken chord pattern in triplet rhythm; however, a careful accompanist should be able to control this tendency. The range and voice leading throughout are all relatively simple and amateur choirs should experience no difficulty with this work.

Piano　　　　　　　　　　　　　　　　　　　c'-g"

Aichinger, Gregor (ed. Clara Tillinghast)　　　　W 2899

"Regina Coeli"

SSA　　　　　　　　　Diff.　　　　　　　　3 min.

This is a very exciting motet in a fairly fast tempo, and totally contrapuntal throughout. Many of the vocal entrances are imitative and the "pyramiding" of such entrances, strategically delayed by divisions of the measure, adds great excitement to the texture. The vocal lines are conceived in simple diatonic fashion; however, an occasional rhythmic syncopation and the high range of both soprano parts contribute somewhat to the difficulty of the work. There is one minor tempo and meter change about halfway through the work, but this is easily made. The only other tempo changes are an occasional ritardando into a strong cadence in which the moving parts still continue to lend rhythmic drive to the cadences. This is certainly an excellent example of contrapuntal style, strong in appeal and vitality.

Unacc.　　　　　　　　　　　　　　　　　　　a-a"

Bach, J. S.　　　　　　　　　　　　　　　　　ESR 813

"Suscepit Israel"
(from the Magnificat)

SSA　　　　　　　Med.-Diff.　　　　　　2-1/2 min.

This excerpt from Bach's Magnificat in D is
scored for only three voices. The music presents a number of difficulties for chorus, yet
is worthy of rehearsal time for any women's
chorus. Except for the duets which appear in
the Cantatas, this and one trio from the motet
Jesu Meine Freude are the only works by Bach
for women's voices. This trio is entirely polyphonic in style and all three vocal lines are
scored in a highly independent manner, usually
following an ascending or descending curve. The
accompaniment is comprised of repeated pulsat-
ing chords which produce a quasi-ostinato effect
throughout the work.

Oboe, BC (or piano or organ)   g-g"

Barber, Samuel   GS 8386
                     "The Virgin Martyrs" (Op. 8)

SSAA   Diff.   3-1/2 min.

This work for women's voices by the American
composer Samuel Barber is a very effective number. A high degree of complex syncopation is evident throughout, made more difficult by the lack
of accompaniment. Harmonically, the work is quite
contemporary in that dissonances are everywhere,
though always resolved. The work contains a number of sections in which imitative vocal lines are
employed; however, the composer often treats two
voices as a unit in contrast to the counterpoint of
the other two voices. This makes the work somewhat easier and brings a sense of unity to the
structure. Tempo changes, meter changes, key
and mood changes abound, all of which contribute
to the variety within the work, and add to the excitement engendered within the music.

Unacc.   g-a^{b}"

Bartók, Béla   Bo Ha 1668
                        "Don't Leave Me"

SA   Easy   1-1/2 min.

This work begins as a two-part canon but devi-
ates from that form following the first sixteen
measures. The two vocal lines are predominantly independent; this would serve as a good selection for an amateur chorus to use in an attempt
to build independence of sections. The text setting is easy, as are the melody lines. The fourth
degree of the scale is raised frequently, thereby
creating a modal shift which must be carefully

observed.

Unacc. or orchestra   b-d''

Bartók, Béla   Bo Ha 1670

"Only Tell Me"

SSA   Med.   2 min.

This is one of the better works of several which
the composer has scored for female voices. The
repetition of the theme is a haunting treatment
and the harmonies created by the chromatic
treatment of the vocal lines are quite interesting. In contrast to many of his other works,
which are highly canonic in structure, this music
has fewer such passages. The work is not too
difficult; however, the vocal parts demand independence of control and good hearing on the part
of the singers. The range is very reasonable.

Unacc. or orchestra   g-e''

Bell, W. H.   Ox 510

"The Flower of Jesse"
(from Four Medieval Songs)

SSA (divisi)   Easy-med.   2 min.

This work is a simple setting of a religious
song. The harmonies are generally simple and
the compositional style is almost entirely homophonic. The accompaniment is predominantly independent of the vocal parts and is also simple
in style.

Piano or strings   a-a''

Berger, Jean   JF 9562

"A Child's Book of Beasts"

SA   Easy   6-7 min.

1. The Yak
2. The Polar Bear
3. The Dromedary
4. The Hippopotamus
5. The Rhinoceros
6. The Frog

This is an imaginative group of clever verses
set simply but effectively for two-part chorus.
The vocal lines are generally easy, but a modern flavor is added by the clever accompaniment,

which is cast in a modern idiom. Each selection
is scored in duet style except number three,
which is a canon. The variation of tempo in the
selections provides good contrast when the group
is performed as a set. The pieces are especially
good to perform before small children. They can
be performed by grade school children, providing
an excellent early experience in singing music of
a contemporary style.

Piano   b^{b}-e''

Brahms, Johannes   N 430

"Adoramus"
(We Adore Thee)

SSAA   Diff.   2 min.

This motet is number two of a set of three sacred
choruses which comprise Op. 37. The harmonies
employed in this work make it more difficult than
the first and last numbers, which may be due to
Brahms' canonic writing in this piece. The first
two-thirds of the work is scored in canonic style.
The first entrance is between the soprano parts
one measure apart, followed by the two alto parts
in like manner, although an extra measure sepa-
rates the paired entrances between sopranos and
altos. The final ten measures of the work are in
strict homophonic style, with no independent counterpoint. This mixture of styles presents an excellent contrast within the work and exemplifies the
versatility of Brahms.

Unacc.   g-a''

Broude 136

Brahms, Johannes   GS 9115

"Ave Maria" (Op. 12)
("Blessed Are They That Dwell in Thy House")

SSAA   Med.   5 min.

This early work by Brahms was probably written
during the composer's brief visit to Gottingen in
1858. The text is part of the liturgical invoca-
tion to the Virgin Mary. The work is completely
homophonic in style and frequent use is made of
passages in consecutive thirds (duet-style) for
voices in pairs (i.e. two sopranos alternating
with two alto parts). Some modulatory passages
occur briefly, but the work is predominantly
melodic in conception. The accompaniment is
quite effective throughout, sometimes doubling

the vocal lines, sometimes completely independent
of them, as in the "Sancta Maria" section where
the voices sing in unison and octave doubling. The
work contains a few brief moments of chromatic
movement which Brahms so often uses, but it is
essentially diatonic and harmonically uncomplex.
The original accompaniment is for orchestra.

Orchestra (or piano)   g-a"

ECS 2515, P 3651

Brahms, Johannes   ECS 2504

"Come Away, Come Away, Death!"
(Komm herbei Tod) (Op. 17, N 2)

SSA   Med.   3 min.

This is a unique piece of music based on a text
by Shakespeare. (On this point, a performance in
English seems perfectly justified.) The work is
not difficult, but the accompaniment by two horns
and harp is necessary to the effectiveness of the
work. The rhythmic motif of the harp is used as
a call by which death is summoned. The harp part
almost always is used in contrasting phrases or
sections against the horns, but almost never with
them. The dotted rhythm pattern used by voices,
harp and horns is perhaps the most difficult aspect
of the work.

Two horns and harp b^b-g"

GS 4301, N. Trios 181

Brahms, Johannes (ed. HC-L)   ECS 1069

"Fidelin!" (Op. 44 N. 3)

SSAA (AA)   Med.   3 min.

This composition begins with a solo-duet by two
alto voices scored in a typical French horn duet
manner. This is immediately answered by the
chorus on the word "Fidelin", whereupon the
two alto soloists take up the next phrase. The
answer follows by the full chorus, which remains singing for the remainder of the verse.
The text is reminiscent of a "boy meets girl"
story, but the musical medium presents the old
theme in a fresh and interesting manner. None
of the chromatic shifts which are so typical of
Brahms are employed in this work; the harmony
sounds much like the manner of a harmonized
folk song. The accompaniment is quite simple
and unobtrusive.

Accomp.   g#-f#"

N 335, UPC 72, Kalmus

Brahms, Johannes   ECS 1627

"Greetings" (Op. 17 N. 3)
(Der Gärtner - The Gardener)

SSA   Med.   4 min.

This is another of the many successful works
that Brahms scored for women's voices with
harp and horns. This work is not difficult for
the vocal or horn parts, although a fairly good
harpist is required to give the proper delicate-
ness to the arpeggio figures. The first soprano
melody is truly beautiful, and Brahms has let it
remain so by not calling any attention to the other
voice parts, which are artistically subdued in complexity. This is a love song in all its splendor and
the English text by Natalie MacFarren is quite
good.

Two horns and harp b^b-$a^{b,,}$

N Trios 182, ECS 2503, GS 4302

Brahms, Johannes   ECS 494

"I Hear A Harp" (Op. 17 N. 1)
(Es tönt ein voller Harfenklang)

SSA   Med.   4 min.

With a good harpist and an average horn player,
this is a most effective number despite relatively simple voice parts. There are dissonances in
the vocal parts to be sure, but all are excellent-
ly prepared and evolved out of the horn accompaniment figure. Long interludes of harp and horn
alone provide interesting contrast to the vocal
sounds. The range of dynamic contrasts within
this piece contributes much to its effectiveness
and serves as a good illustration of the Romantic
temperament.

Horn and harp   d'-g''

N Trios 180, GS 4300

Brahms, Johannes   N 429

"O Bone Jesu" (Op. 37 N. 1)

SSA   Med.   1-1/2 min.

This sacred work by Brahms, the first of a set
of three sacred choruses in his Opus 37, is a
Latin motet, not unlike the homophonic motets
of Roselli and Palestrina, although the harmonic

idiom is quite different. This is a rather strik-
ing work in devotional style, but whatever its
affinity with the earlier Palestrina manner of
writing, there is no mistaking it as Brahms,
due largely to the rich nineteenth-century harmonies. The work involves frequent voice crossings and
a beautifully scored section of resolving suspensions during the final seven measures which is
strongly reminiscent of similar passages in the
Requiem.

Unacc.   f-g"

Broude 136

Brahms, Johannes   431

"Queen of the Heavens" (Op. 37. N. 3)
(Regina Coeli)

SSAA (SA)   Diff.   3-1/2 min.

This is an excellent work written in quite an
unusual style for Brahms. The work is much
more in the style of Haydn, quite diatonic, with
ample florid scale passages. The piece begins
with an inverted canonic effect in contrary mo-
tion by the two soloists. The chorus joins in a
responsorial "Halleluia" which sets the style for
a good half of the number. The chorus, however,
soon takes up its role of delivering the text and
the work ends with both chorus and soloists pro-
claiming ecstatic "Halleluias".

Unacc.   g-g"

Brahms, Johannes (ed. HC-L)   ECS 1072

"Roses Are Blooming" (Op. 44 N. 7)
(Rosen in Blüthe)

SSAA   Diff.   2-1/2 min.

This piece by Brahms, composed as number
seven in a set of twelve lieder and "romanzen",
is a typical example of Brahms' writing for women's voices. The tempo marking of allegro is
perhaps misleading, as the work should be performed as a lilting waltz. The English words
leave much to be desired and the original German text is highly preferable. The harmonic
treatment and idiomatic writing are strictly
Brahms. Frequent use of chromatic voice leading (and occasional chord shifts) combined with
contrasting sections of unison (or octave doubling)
melody offer artistic relief and effectively highlight the text. The accompaniment is primarily
used in a supportive role.

Piano   f#-g#"

JF 4881, Kalmus, P 3669b, UPC 73

Brahms, Johannes   338

"The Nun" (Op. 44 N. 6)
(Die Nonne)

SSAA   Med.   3 min.

This is an exceptionally beautiful work, simply
and effectively scored. The work is strophic in
form and the harmonization and vocal writing
are scored accordingly except for the last verse,
in which Brahms shifts from minor tonality to
major in an extended (or augmented) terce di
picardi effect. The accompaniment is indicated
ad lib., and the work can certainly be performed without it. However, it is an effective accompaniment and there is no reason to omit it.
It is of particular aid in supplying the occasional
low sonority often needed in music for women's
voices.

Piano ad lib.   g-g"

Kalmus, P 3669a

Brahms, Johannes   ECS 1055

"Three Love Songs"

SA   Med.   3 min.

1. Like The Sunset's Crimson Splendor (Op. 52 N. 4)
   (Wie des Abends Schöne Röte)   1 min.
2. Bird in Air Will Stray Afar (Op. 52 N. 13)
   (Völgelein Durch-rauscht die Luft)   1 min.
3. Set Thyself, My Dearest Heart (Op. 65 N. 13)
   (Mein Geliebter, Setze Dich)   1 min.

These love waltzes are similar in style to the
famous Liebeslieder waltzes. None of them is
difficult, and the refreshing waltz tempos make
them a joy and pleasure to sing. All the duets
contain elements of chromaticism, the third being
the most difficult. Numbers one and three are not
difficult rhythmically, but the second duet includes
elements of syncopation which might offer some
problems to the amateur choir. All three duets
are worthy of serious attention by conductors and
are not unduly difficult; however, the accompaniment will require two good pianists.

Piano (4 hands)   a#-a^{b}"

UPC 111-112

Brahms, Johannes   ECS 1530

"True Lover's Heart" (Op. 66 N. 1)
(Klänge)

SA   Med.   2 min.

This is a modestly presented duet which can
nevertheless be quite effective when well performed. It is most important that the tempo
be not fast, but carefully established to maintain consistency with the text. The rhythm of
the voice parts occasionally becomes a little
complex and this is the only potential difficulty
of the work. There is little non-diatonic chromaticism and no difficult harmonic shifts. This
could be considered almost an easy number, except for the slight rhythm problems mentioned
and a fairly difficult (and important) piano accompaniment.

Piano   d'-g''

Britten, Benjamin   Bo Ha

"A Ceremony of Carols" (Op. 23)

SSA (SS)   Med.   20 min.

Originally composed for boys' treble voices,
this work has come to be a standard part of
the repertoire for women's choral groups.
The text is in Old English, lending a medieval
flavor to the work. This collection of nine
carols begins and ends with an early Gregorian
melody sung by unison choir and indicated as
Processional and Recessional. The accompaniment throughout is for harp, and when the
carols are performed as a group (as an extended work) there is a long harp solo (interlude) mid-point in the work. The variations in
style, tempos and text of the carols provide
effective contrasts. The harmonies are modern,
but not particularly difficult. The rhythms are not
too difficult, but the solos are more challenging.
The writing style employed is essentially of a modern homophonic character; however three of the
carols employ canonic imitation. This composition is
worthy of almost any amount of rehearsal necessary
for a good performance.

Harp (or piano) [expert needed] a^b-a''

Britten, Benjamin

"Old Abram Brown"

SSAA   Easy   1-1/2 min.

The effect of this number is that of a round and
indeed it is handled in that style for the most
part. It is a delightful number, short, but much
fun to sing, and the piano accompaniment adds a
great deal of interest and contrast to the musical
treatment. There is considerable independence of
parts when all four vocal sections are busy with
the canonic imitation, but it is an easy number to
perform.

Piano   e'-e''

Buxtehude, Dietrich   Bärenreiter-Ausgabe 3625

"Nun Freut Euch Ihr Frommem Mit Mir"
(Cantata)

SS (SS)   Easy   12 min.

This is a little-known work of Buxtehude, worthy
of the attention of choral directors or voice teachers. It may be performed by a chorus or by two
solo voices. When the two vocal lines are inter-
changed (or inverted) during two brief passages,
the work can also be performed by soprano and
alto (chorus or soloists). The cantata contains
two duets (the opening and closing sections) and
two arias, one for soprano I, the other for
soprano II. The work begins with an Instrumental
Sonata, scored for two violins and basso continuo,
and each of the four remaining sections, except
the last, closes with an orchestral ritornello. This
is a good example of early cantata style. It contains many sections of canonic counterpoint, as
well as numerous passages which represent duet-
style writing of this early Baroque period.

2 Violins and BC   d'-b''

Byrd, William   ECS 855

"Rejoice!   Rejoice!"

SSAA (A)   Diff.   3-1/2 min. total
                                                 1-1/2 min. chor. section

This work is divided into two sections, the first
being an alto solo with organ or string accompaniment, and set to Francis Kinwelmersh's text
"From Virgin pure this day did spring" authored
in 1576. The second part of the work is a highly
complex polyphonic chorus in four parts, which
may be performed alone without the preceding
alto solo. When so performed, no accompaniment
is used. The alto solo is comprised of long sustained phrases supported by the accompaniment,

which is also interspersed between the phrases
in the style of the Bach "extended chorales".
The chorus section which follows is an exciting
contrapuntal composition employing imitative
entrances. A change of tempo and meter halfway through begins a new section in a short
homophonic passage, followed immediately by
a return to the polyphonic style with which the
work opened. The counterpoint is complex and
the rhythmic phrases across the measures may
present some difficulties in early readings.

Organ or string accomp.   g-g"
unacc. choral section

Caplet, Andre'   Durand

"Messe a Trois Voix"

SSA   Diff.   20 min.

This full-length work is in a typical French
idiom and contains some fine lyric sections.
The long melismatic phrases on occasion are
difficult, requiring great vocal control in their
execution. Much of the part writing is also difficult and contains a fair degree of chromaticism. In addition to some beautiful moments of
melodic writing, there are contrasting dynamic
sections which are very exciting. The work
abounds in rhythmic, tempo, dynamic and harmonic changes, all of which add great interest
to the composition in general. The traditional
sections of the mass are included.

Unacc.   g-a^{b}"

Chabrier, Emmanuel   BM

"The Shulamite"

SSAA (MS)   Diff.   18 min.

This work of extended length by Chabrier is
quite modern in its use of tonalities and the
vocal lines contain many chromatic passages.
In addition, the composer has employed many
rhythmic figures which add to the complexity
of the composition. There are numerous passages in which triplet figures are preceded or
followed by duple figures in the same vocal
line. These figures also are used simultane-
ously in two or more vocal parts. The accompaniment material is no less difficult,
nor are the mezzo soprano solo sections,
which are also rather extensive. Frequent
changes of time signature and tempo also

occur throughout the work. The work is a dramatic
composition which should be considered only by the
most advanced choral groups.

Orchestra (or piano)   g-b^{b}''

Couperin, Francois   Mercury MC 14
          "Troisième Leçon de Ténèbres"
          (Lamentation of Jeremiah 1:10-14)
SS (SS)   Diff.   10 min.

This is a work worthy of serious consideration by
any advanced vocal ensemble. The general frame-
work is that of alternating text assignments between solo voice and the two-part chorus. Some
of the solo sections are set in recitative style,
others in aria style. The result is a miniature
dramatic work of the highest order. The chorus
parts are frequently scored in two-part imitative
counterpoint and the sequential suspensions which
often result are especially effective. Neither the
solo sections nor the chorus parts are difficult in
themselves; however, the addition of the suggested
vocal ornaments adds considerable challenge to
those who would consider a more authentic performance. The continuo part is quite traditional,
yet often provides a third melodic line to the
texture. It cannot be omitted. However, the string
parts could be performed by organ, harpsichord
or piano.

BC (str. ad lib.)   c'-g''

Crichton, Margaret   Cur 71762
                "Fear No More"
SSA   Med.   2-1/2 min.

This is a very worthwhile number which has been
neglected in most bibliographic listings. The text
is by Shakespeare and the melody is strongly
reminiscent of Vaughn Williams or an English
folk melody. The work is predominantly homophonic, although it contains a few brief moments
of imitative entrances. The whole idiomatic style
of the work is that of a folk song.

Unacc.   a^{b}-g''

Cui, Cesar Antonovitch (ed. HC-L)   BM 715
                "Mystic Chorus"
                (Chorus Mysticus)
SSA   Diff.   5 min.

This work by the famed Russian composer may
be considered almost a lament. It is a powerful
work which would probably appeal only to more
mature choirs and audiences. The vocal parts
are highly independent, but not so much in a
polyphonic manner, for the work must be regarded as homophonic in style. The work is not too
demanding technically; its difficulty lies rather
in the profundity of the text and its musical
means. The accompaniment is not difficult, but is effective. Some passages in the first part of the work
are scored without accompaniment.

Orchestra (or piano)   g-a"

Debussy, Claude   GS

"The Blessed Damozel"

SSAA (SMS)   Med.   20 min.

Following Debussy's winning of the Prix de Rome
in 1884 for his cantate L'Enfant Prodigue, he sub-
mitted The Blessed Damozel to the Section des
Beaux Arts, where it was promptly rejected by
the judges for what they termed its unorthodoxy.
Actually, the work may be regarded as a master-
piece. Compared with his later works there is
little of the unorthodox use of whole-tone and
pentatonic scales. The poem by Rossetti is of the
highest order, although the English translation
does not do justice to Debussy's music. Nevertheless, it is worthy of being performed in either
language. The solo sections present more of a
challenge than the choral sections, being far more
difficult. All of the choral sections are homophonic,
and many are scored for unison chorus. The accompaniment is quite difficult and calls for a skillful and sensitive pianist.

Piano   f-a"

Dello Joio, Norman   GS 9672

"A Jubilant Song"

SSAA (S)   Diff.   6 min.

This work, originally composed for mixed voices,
has long been one of the best known of Dello
Joio's compositions. This setting for women's
voices has been arranged by the composer and
little if anything has been lost from the original.
It is a brilliant and exciting piece of music, not
the least significant part of which is the aggressive and driving piano accompaniment, which demands an excellent accompanist. The vocal sections

are marked with a great deal of parallel movement in the voices, which are often paired off
in alternating passages. The text, adapted from
Walt Whitman, is infused with great rhythmic
vitality and necessitates frequent shifts of meter.
Full rich harmonies are contrasted with frequent
sections of unison and octave-doubling sections,
while a beautiful cantabile soprano solo (supported
by rich choral chords) adds further variety to the
work. Tempo and dynamic contrasts are abundant.

Piano   g-g#"

Dello Joio, Norman   Marks 4307

"Song's End"

SSA   Diff.   3-1/2 min.

This work was commissioned by the Women's
Glee Club of the State University College at
Oneonta, New York on the occasion of the college's Seventy-fifth Anniversary. Dello Joio has
scored several passages of poly-tonality and poly-
rhythm in this setting of the John Payne text.
Frequently, there are difficult intervals in the
voice parts, and a number of meter changes occur between 4/4, 5/4 and 6/8. The accompaniment is predominantly independent of the vocal
lines and employs a generous amount of modern,
and sometimes dissonant, chords. Except for
one or two brief sections the work is not homophonic, yet it cannot be considered as polyphonic
either. The vocal lines maintain a consistent independence throughout, and each is conceived
melodically, with only occasional consideration
for vertical harmonic results.

Piano   b-a"

Des Prés, Josquin   WLSM

"Ave Verum"

SSA   Easy   1-1/2 min.

There are few easily available works of this
early master for women's (or equal) voices.
This publication not only makes such a work
available, but it is an excellent example of
the early Renaissance style of this important
composer. The motet begins with the first section scored for SA only, the compositional style
being that of imitative counterpoint. This soon
changes to a writing style in which the soprano
line sings longer melismas over sustained tones
in the alto. Near the close of this first section,

both parts are scored in a more homophonic style. The second half of the work is in three voice texture, and the writing style is predominantly that of three-part polyphony.

Unacc.   f-f''

Destouches, A. G. (Trans. Auguste Chapuis)   BM 686
                    "Shepherd Song"
                    (Gentils Bergers)

SSA   Easy   2 min.

This is a simple treatment of a quite nice lilting melody. The work begins with a "la'la" presentation of the main musical material followed by two verses in strophic-type presentation of the same basic material. An accompaniment by Arthur Ryder has been added, but is not necessary to the performance. The vocal treatment is predominantly homophonic, although the alto part is occasionally treated independently, but simply. The whole nature of the work is much like a folk song.

Accom.   a-e''

Diemer, Emm Lou   Marks 96
                "Fragments from the Mass"

SSAA   Med.   6 min.

    I   Kyrie
   II Gloria
  III Credo
  IV Sanctus
   V Agnus Dei

A short mass, in semi-modern idiom, this work contains a considerable degree of variety in the movements. The opening and closing sections employ the same musical material and harmonizations throughout, and are set in a moderately slow tempo with the emphasis on melodic expression. This is true of the Credo section as well. The Gloria and the second part of the Sanctus sections are scored in a more exciting fashion in terms of faster tempos and more rhythmic complexities, and both employ some counterpoint. The Sanctus includes a sustained alto pedal point effect throughout the first half, over which the upper two voices are scored in duet style. The entire work has a modern "flavor" associated with the harmonies. The main performance problems will be found in the

rhythmic syncopations which occur in all but one
of the sections.

Unacc.   g-g''

Duruflé, Maurice   Durand

"Tota pulchra es"
(from Coll. Quatre Motets)

SSA (divisi)   Med.   2 min.

Based on a Gregorian theme, this is a delightful
motet in the contemporary idiom by the French
composer Duruflé, who has also scored an excellent Requiem Mass for mixed voices. This motet
contains frequent metrical shifts, all easily handled.
While much of the musical material is fully composed, the rondo strophic treatment of the original
chant is evident and used to good effect. While
much of the effect is chordal, each of the parts is
treated independently with much interesting material in the inner voices.

Unacc.   g-a''

Este, Michael (rev. G. Holst)   GS 5359

"How Merrily We Live"

SSA   Med.   2 min.

There is excellent vocal training value in singing
madrigals, but equally important is that choral
groups (especially those of women's voices) find
them great fun to sing. This madrigal by Este
is an appropriate example of late sixteenth-century madrigal style. It is based on imitation
among the three vocal lines, with many passages
in which two of the parts are scored in duet fashion. These imitative sections are contrasted with
brief moments of pure homophony, and together
the two styles provide logical contrasts in style
and form. The selection is diatonic and presents
no harmonic or rhythmic difficulties; however,
independently strong chorus sections are essential for a good performance. The melodic material in all voice parts is highly singable, and the
overall result is that the work sounds quite easy.

Unacc.   a-f#''

ECS 1062

Fauré, Gabriel (ed. EHG)   ESV 860

"Ave Verum"
(Jesu, Word of God Incarnate)

SA   Med.   2 min.

> This is a simple, unpretentious motet in two
> parts, most of which is alternating phrases and
> sections between the two voice parts. The vocal
> phrases are highly melodic, and despite their
> length, are easily sung. The organ accompani-
> ment is also unpretentious and simply conceived,
> but in typical Fauré manner, it adds much rich-
> ness of harmony and color to the effect of the
> work. A change in tonality from F minor to F
> major halfway through provides interesting variety
> to the work, as the accompaniment style also
> changes at this section.

Organ   a-f''

Fauré, Gabriel   ESV 681

"Tantum Ergo" (Op. 65 N. 2)
(Therefore We Before Him Bending)

SSA (SSA)   Med.   2-1/2 min.

> This work is set in strict homophonic style in
> the use of both chorus and soloists. The solo-
> ists' parts are scored as trio sections, as well
> as independent solo sections. It is possible to
> perform the work without the use of soloists by
> assigning the chorus to these sections. The work
> begins with a trio for the three soloists, followed
> by a short two-measure solo pattern being repeat-
> ed. (There is no solo passage anywhere for the
> alto solo voice.) The work concludes with an alter-
> nating "Amen" section between the trio of soloists
> and the chorus. The accompaniment role is strict-
> ly that of supporting the vocal parts.

Organ   g#-g''

Broude

Gerrish, John   AMP A-295

"A Virgin Most Pure"

SSA (SSA)   Med.   4 min.

> This is an excellent Christmas number which is
> set in alternating major and minor tonalities and
> constructed with alternating solo duet and chorus
> sections, which greatly enhance the beautiful tra-
> ditional text. The first sporano part is quite easy;
> however, the two lower parts are filled with dif-
> ficult interval changes caused by the shifts be-
> tween major and minor tonality. While the accom-
> paniment is predominantly independent and adds
> to the effect of the work, it nevertheless supports

much of the vocal material, especially in the harmonic sections where such support is needed. In
other places, it provides rhythmic contrast which
is a welcome addition to the pulsation of the vocal
material.

Piano   g-e''

Gevaert, François (ed. EHG)   ESV 868

"O Filli et Filiae"
(O ye sons and daughters)

SSA   Easy-Med.   2 min.

This is a famous text which has been set by many
composers. Gavaert has assigned the first three
verses to each of the three vocal sections as solo
passages, with the "Alleluia" refrain being scored
for full chorus between each of the three verses.
Each of the three solo assignments is set to a different melody, with the only repeated material
being the "Alleluia". The final verse begins with
unison chorus and employs the first melody for
its text. The "Alleluia" section is used again to
close out the work. Diatonic throughout, the work's
only difficult aspect is the rhythmic syncopation
presented in each of the four verses.

Unacc.   a-f''

Gibbs, C. Armstrong   Ox 2230

"O, Praise God in His Holiness"
(Psalm CL)

SA   Med.   2-1/2 min.

This is a stirring and very impressive anthem
which the composer wrote especially for the 1953
Festival of the Federation of Essex (England) Women's Institutes in honor of Queen Elizabeth II's
coronation. The work begins on a five-note theme
in the accompaniment, which is taken up by the
choir in unison, and which returns in various
keys throughout the work. The scoring contains
much unison, as well as excellent part writing
in which extremes of power are contrasted with
pure melodic lyricism. The accompaniment is
quite independent and dramatic throughout the
work, and dynamic contrasts both in accompaniment and chorus parts are plentiful and well
handled.

Piano, organ or
orchestra   c'-g''

Haines, Edmund   Broude

"Dialogue from the Book of Job"
(In Memoriam November 22, 1963)

SSAA (SA)   Diff.   8 min.

This composition was commissioned by Harold
Aks and the Sarah Lawrence Chorus in memory
of President John F. Kennedy. Haines is a member of the faculty at Sarah Lawrence College and
has been a recipient of a Pulitzer Prize and two
Guggenheim Fellowships. This is an extremely
difficult work, mainly due to the large amount of
dissonant effects created in the vocal parts and
also in the accompaniment. More acute is the
problem of large, angular intervals within each
vocal line, and extremes of ranges which the composer scores. Difficult rhythms and disjunct melismas occur frequently in the vocal lines. The accompaniment is usually independent of the vocal
line, and is frequently treated as another ensemble which contrasts with the vocal sections.
The work also contains several sections for
speaking chorus against solo passages.

Piano   f-b"

Handel, Georg Friedrich (ed. HC-L)   ESC 1039

"O Lovely Peace, with Plenty Crowned"
(from Judas Maccabaeus)

SA   Med.   3 min.

This pastoral-type duet is a fine example of two-
part writing in the late Baroque period. The piano accompaniment establishes both the mood and
the musical material for the vocal writing which
follows. The vocal material begins with a long
statement by the soprano alone, followed by a
similar length section by the alto voice, using
the same text. The two voices then take up the
lovely duet material which forms most of the remainder of the work. A closing ritornello by the
piano rounds off the selection in the traditional
Baroque aria pattern.

Piano   c'-f"

Handel, Georg Friedrich   Cur 70841

"Come Ever Smiling Liberty"
(from Judas Maccabaeus)

SS   Easy   1-1/2 min.
or SA

This is a simple duet from Handel's Oratorio
Judas Maccabaeus that is delightful and interesting to sing. The work begins with a canonic imitation between the two voice parts, which is then
resolved into typical Baroque duet-style writing.
There are a number of short sequentially treated
phrases between the two voice parts which give
the piece interest from the standpoint of independence within each voice part; simple but effective. The accompaniment is not difficult, but
must be performed with clarity and knowledge of
the "thorough-bass" style.

Accomp.   d'-e''

N School 21

Handel, Georg Friedrich   GS 150

"The Smiling Dawn"
(from Jeptha)

SSA   Med.   3 min.

This chorus from Handel's Oratorio Jeptha is in
typical Handelian fashion, employing homophony
and sprinkled with occasional phrases of polyphonic imitation. The Bouree-type tempo gives
the work a lilting joyousness which adequately
captures the gaiety and lightness of the text.
There are several sections in which the composer scores a florid sequential melody to a
single syllable, usually in one voice part at a
time. There are also a number of phrase sections in which two paired voices are featured
while the third voice is temporarily unscored.
As in the case of the vocal parts, the accompaniment is quite simple and is used mainly to
support and double the voice parts.

Piano (orig. orch.)   a-g''

Handl (Gallus), Jacob (ed. P. Boepple)   Mercury DCS 31

"Replenti Sunt Omnes"

SSAA-SSAA   Easy-Med.   1-1/2 min.
(double choir)

This is a fine example of the double choir work
for which Handl has become so well known. It
is scored for two choirs of equal voices in predominantly homophonic style. The two choirs
alternate brief choral passages, usually repeating the text just previously sung. Overlapping
of these sections is effectively achieved by having one of the choirs begin a new section while
the opposite choir is just completing a phrase.

There are no difficult rhythms, no meter changes.
The chord progressions are all diatonic in a minor
tonality (except the final "terce di picardy" chord).
This would be a reasonably easy introduction to
antiphonal choir singing, an experience which is
quite exciting to the amateur singer.

Unacc.   f-a"

Harris, Roy   GS 8503

"Whitman Triptych"

SSSSA   1. "I Hear America Singing"   2 min.
SSA   2. "An Evening Lull"   1 min.
SSAA   3. "America"   2-1/2 min.

Diff.

These works by Harris are quite different from
the usual choral music to be found. The first
number for example has no text, but simply an
alternating of "oh" and "ah". At least half of
the selection is nothing more than an alternating
among the four soprano parts of phrases set in
unison, although cleverly scored in a smooth
"hocketing" fashion. The second number contains a considerable amount of dissonance, much
of it unresolved, but employing text throughout.
A slight change of tempo is also included. The
third selection begins with the "oh" - "ah" al-
ternation of the first number, but the text is
soon introduced. This number is comprised of
both homophony and counterpoint and is the most
difficult of the three, as the four parts are quite
independent. Several tempo, meter, and mood
changes endow this with considerably more variety than the preceding numbers of the set.

Unacc.   g-a"

Hasse, Johann Adolf (ed. Hugo Leichtentritt)   GS

"Miserere"
(Psalm LI)

SSAA (SAA)   Diff.   20 min.

Known primarily as a composer of operas, Hasse
was one of the musical celebrities of the eighteenth century. The Miserere was written in 1728 for
the girls' chorus and ensemble of the Conserva-
torio degl' Incurabili, an orphan asylum and hos-
pital in Venice. The work is comprised of six
major sections: three for chorus, two for soprano
solo and one for alto duet. The choral sections
are a mixture of homophony and polyphony with

passages in two-part duet style in each of the
chorus sections. The solo and duet sections are
much in the style of the solos and duets of the
Bach Cantatas or Handel Oratorios. The orchestral material (or piano accompaniment) is
generally quite independent of the vocal material
in the treatment of the melodic portions, although
it is supportive of the harmonies in the choral
sections.

Strings or piano   g-g''

Hodge, Talbot   Ch 6712
                         "Cuckoo Song"

SS   Med.   2 min.

This work is quite impressive and generally simple
to perform. Both the accompaniment and the echoing between the two voice parts contribute to the
traditional "cuckoo" concept of musical settings
dealing with this favorite musical bird. There
are, of course, sections with considerable independence of parts, but this is artistically contrasted with a reasonable amount of two-part harmonic writing. An occasional shift from 4/4 to
3/4 meter wisely avoids rhythmic monotony. Except for a few intervals which may be a little difficult to hear on first readings, this is a relatively simple piece.

Accomp.   c'-f#''

Holst, G.   Cur 8792
                    "A Dream of Christmas"

SA   Easy   3 min.

This simple setting by Holst of Mary Segar's
beautiful text from her "Medieval Anthology" is
a significantly unusual number. The melodic pattern is in Dorian mode for the first half of the
selection, and this is most effective in capturing
the beauty of the text. Much of this selection is
in unison, although the refrain-like section is
scored in simple two-part writing following each
of five short verses. The accompaniment is quite
simple and serves only to reinforce and support
the vocal line, although it does contribute significantly to the modal harmonies. Both the text
and the modality employed contribute to making
this an exceptionally fine Christmas number
which is refreshingly different. The basic structure is that of two three-measure phrases followed by two four-measure phrases.

Accomp.   d'-d''

Holst, Gustave   Gray 312

"Ave Maria"

SSAA-SSAA   Med.   4-1/2 min.
(double chorus)

> This is a motet composed for double chorus,
> which the composer dedicated to the memory
> of his mother. The work is in slow tempo and
> homophonic style, but is difficult because of
> its wide range and the difficult interval skips
> which often occur within the inner voices. Much
> of the vocal movement is of a scale nature,
> which results in sections of rich harmony and
> poignant dissonances. The work is unaccom-
> panied and as a result, there is an excellent
> interplay between the two choruses, which
> Holst treats equally in importance. This should
> be a very challenging work for the more mature
> choir.

Unacc.   f-b^{b}''

Holst, Gustave   Gray 286

(from Choral Hymns from the Rig Veda)
Group II
No. 3 "Funeral Chant" (Op. 26)

SSSAAA   Med.   3 min.

> This third number in the second group of Holst's
> Opus 26 is a most unique selection. The work
> is based entirely on an eight-note chant, which
> the composer treats very effectively. With the
> devices of parallelism, canonic imitation, frag-
> mentation and augmentation, he has created a
> most impressive piece of music. The accompani-
> ment also employs the chant theme modestly, and
> in addition creates a sustained descending scale
> passage in the bass which is very effective. The
> difficulties of performance are centered in the
> medieval-type parallelism which constitutes the
> main portion of the work and in the canonic en-
> trances of the divisi voice parts.

Piano   g-g''

Holst, G.   APS 421

"Four Old English Carols"

SSAA (SA)   Med.   1-1/2 min. each

1. A Babe is born

2. Now let us sing
3. Jesus, thou the virgin-born (no accompaniment)
4. In Bethlehem, that noble place

Each of these four choral carols by the English master is fresh and unhackneyed. Some hint of modal flavor appears in each of the carols, and the words are mainly from the fifteenth century. Piano accompaniment is featured in numbers two and four and lends exceptional importance to the harmonies of the carols. (Number four is scored for unison voice.) Contrasts of tempo, line signature, rhythm and key make the set an interesting unit to be performed as a group, although each is sufficient to be performed alone. Of Swedish origin, but born in England, Holst has completely adapted himself to the English style of composition, as these carols clearly testify.

Accomp. a^b-$e^{b''}$

Holst, G.   SB 1988

"Hecuba's Lament" (Op. 31 N. 1)
(from the Trojan Women of Euripides)

SSAA (SMS or A)   Diff.   10 min.

This is a very difficult, unusual work for women's voices. In addition to the chorus parts which alternate between full harmony and many unison passages, the work calls for a soprano soloist and a mezzo soprano (or alto) soloist in the lead role who possesses an excellent range (g-f''). This perhaps is the main cause of the work's neglect. While it is possible to perform the work with piano alone, it is more effective when accompanied by orchestra. The voice parts, while not too difficult harmonically, contain difficult rhythms and time signatures, which are often unfamiliar (and hence, uncertain) to amateur singers. The work requires an excellent accompanist, but nevertheless is worthy of serious consideration by advanced choirs.

Orch, or piano & str. quintet
(or piano alone)

Holst, G.   SB 1633

"Hymn to Dionysus"
(from The Bacche of Euripides) (Op. 31 N. 2)

SSAA   Diff.   12 min.

This work is even more difficult than Op. 31 N. 2 ("Hecuba's Lament") and really demands a

virtuoso choral group. After a sixteen-measure
orchestral introduction, the chorus begins a long
section of highly syncopated unison singing. There
are a few brief returns to unison scoring, but for
the most part the scoring is in parts, quite difficult and interesting in their dissonant treatment.
Frequent tempo and meter changes are common in
this work, as is constant syncopation which produces interesting and difficult rhythms. The accompaniment is scored for orchestra, but may be
performed with either piano and string quintet or
piano alone, with obvious reduced effect.

Orch. or piano & str. quintet   a-b^{b}"
(or piano alone)

Holst, Gustave   N 514

"Love on My Heart from Heaven Fell"
(Op. 44 N. 6)

SSSA (S)   Med.   2 min.

This work, one of seven part songs in Holst's
Op. 44, is perhaps more difficult than it appears, but should not be too hard for the average choir. The text by Robert Bridges is set
artistically by Holst, somewhat in a folk song
style. The work begins with a soprano solo, the
melody of which is then taken up by the choir in
imitative treatment, prior to a homophonic section in which the voice parts move quite independently. A short interlude for strings precedes
a unison section for chorus which, except for one
measure in harmony, closes the statement of the
vocal phrase by strings. This is worthwhile, and
not too difficult a selection.

Strings or piano   a-g"

Hovhaness, Alan   AMP A-277

"Ave Maria"
(from Triptych)

SSAA   Med.   3 min.

The abbreviated traditional text is set in a not-
too-difficult modern idiom, the effect of which is
enhanced considerably by the original instrumental
scoring. Following a five-measure instrumental
introduction, the four voices take up the text "Ave
Maria" in a modern homophonic style of chordal
changes, with an occasional melismatic line in the
first soprano. No other words are sung, only "Ave
Maria". At measure twenty-five, the texture shifts
to a polyphonic imitative counterpoint. For a brief

episode following, three of the four voices employ melismas before the choral parts return to
the opening homophonic style. The accompaniment is largely doubling of the vocal lines or
sustained chords which create interesting tonal
colors. The closing section is made up of long
sustained chords beneath a melismatic soprano
line. Simple shifts between 3/2 and 2/2 meter
are used throughout.

2 Oboes, 2 horns & harp   g-a''
(or 2 trumpets, 2 trombones & piano)

Ingegneri, Marc Antonio   ECS 1506

"Vere Languores Nostros"
(Surely He hath borne our griefs)

SSA   Med.   1 min.

This is an exceptionally short Latin motet; a
very beautiful example of sixteenth-century
fusion of homophonic and polyphonic style.
Ingegneri was choirmaster at the Cathedral at
Cremona, where he had the great distinction
of having the now-celebrated Claudio Monteverdi as his pupil. For many years, his works
were ascribed erroneously to Palestrina, including this Responsorium (motet). This work is
delicate and simple in its vocal lines; however,
its contrapuntal nature and flowing melodic
curves need a mature approach to performance.

Unacc. a^b-e^{b}''

Kodály, Zoltán   Bo Ha 1711

"Ave Maria"

SSA   Med.   2 min.

Many settings of this familiar text exist for all
types of vocal combinations, but surely none is
more effective than this modern setting by Kodály.
The first part of the work is scored for alto voice
in an almost chant-like intoning of the familiar
text, while the upper two voices enter in an echo
effect at the end of each phrase with the words
"Ave Maria". The latter sections of the work
employ a different technique. Here the upper
voices begin in duet fashion, while the lower
voice continues independently. The closing section of the work begins with an independence of
vocal lines, sometimes imitative in style. The
dissonances and harmonies are quite rich in the
second half of the piece and the overall effect is
highly impressive.

Unacc.   g-g"

Kodály, Zoltán   Bo Ha 1890

"Cease Your Bitter Weeping"

SSA (divisi)   Med.   4-1/2 min.

Based on a religious song or hymn, this has
been set most effectively by Kodály. Each vocal
line, while contributing to some unusual harmony
effects, is treated almost totally as a melody.
Frequent changes of meter are employed to give
the most natural pulse to the text. These are
not difficult changes, and recur in a sequence
pattern so that they actually become easy. The
text is the weakest aspect of the work, in that
the syncopations originally scored by the composer do not always coincide with the translated
text. There are some excellent dynamic contrasts
built into the selection, and the added differentia-
tions between syncopation and sostenuto sections
are artfully placed. The harmonies are not unduly
difficult, although there is frequent shifting of
modal patterns both melodically and harmonically.

Unacc.   d-g"

Kodály, Zoltán (ed. WGW)   Ox 550

"King Ladislaus' Men"
(Magyars and Germans)

SSAA   Diff.   4 min.

This is a rather unusual work, being based on
Hungarian traditional rhythms and melodic frag-
ments which the composer has combined in an
exciting way. The work is scored in dialogue
form as if between the Magyar people and the
German people--a debate about a bridge. The
English text is given, and undoubtedly lends
humorous understanding to the work, but the
music is far more rich and exciting when sung
in the original text. The work is full of syncopated rhythmic motives, which are not easy, but
the melodic patterns are essentially only two.
They are combined in rhythmic, parallel and
contrapuntal ways to produce a sensation of
great complexity. Tempo and mood changes provide considerable variety.

Unacc.   g-a^b"

Kodály, Zoltán (ed. WGW)   Ox 541

"The Deaf Boatman"

SSA   Easy   1-1/2 min.

> This is a humorous song based on a popular Hun-
> garian text. The work is scored in such a way
> that practically any choir can perform it easily.
> There are a few sections of parallel fifths and,
> except for the last few measures, the rest of the
> work is scored in unison, or major thirds. The
> text is a purported conversation between a boatman
> and his boat. The work is quite diatonic and therefore
> easy to sing. Some aspects of syncopation in the
> rhythm might cause amateur choirs some slight dif-
> ficulties during first readings.

Unacc.   g-f#''

Lasso, Orlando di   Bank #2

                              "Adoramus Te"

SSA   Easy-Med.   1 min.

> Of the many settings of this text, this version by
> di Lasso is one of the simplest. A reasonable
> amount of homophonic style is included, so that
> the work is comprised of a mixture of imitative
> and chordal styles. This setting contains no melo-
> dic or harmonic problems; however, the few melis-
> mas contain some rhythmic variation. A few fleet-
> ing suggestions of easy key change identify the
> work as being slightly modal. These modality
> changes are minor and untroublesome, yet present
> an interesting harmonic variety within the selec-
> tion.

Unacc.   b^b-g''

Lasso, Orlando di (ed. EHG)   ESV 890

                      "Adoramus Te Christe"
                    ("We Adore Thee, O Lord")
                (from Magnum Opus Musicum No. 177)

SSSAA   Diff.   1-1/2 min.

> Di Lasso set this text to music on several dif-
> ferent occasions, but this setting is the most
> complex and masterful. Considerable crossing
> of voices is characteristic. The constant over-
> lapping of phrases resulting from masterful
> counterpoint provides an excellent example of
> the high degree of development which the poly-
> phonic style had achieved during this period,
> especially in the hands of this great tonal mas-
> ter. With its intricate polyphonic web and fre-
> quent shifting between major and minor tonal-
> ities, this is an exceptionally beautiful expres-
> sion of reverence.

Unacc.   a-f''

Lasso, Orlando di (ed. Paul Boepple)   Mercury MC 11

"Cantiones Duarum Vocum"
(Magnum Opus I-XX)

SS (or SA)   Med.   1-2 min. each

Twelve Motets for Two Equal Voices

1. Beatus Vir   7. Justi Tulerunt Spolia
2. Beatus Homo   8. Sancti Mei
3. Oculos Non Vidit   9. Qui Vult Venire
4. Justus Cor Suum Tradet   10. Serve Bone
5. Exspectatio Justorum   11. Fulgebunt Justi
6. Qui Sequitur Me   12. Sicut Rosa

These famous motets for two voices are among
24 such compositions which the composer scored.
The other 12 are textless and presumably for
instruments. These are all excellent examples of
two-part counterpoint, often of the imitative type,
but often including less strict contrapuntal technique. Each is a complete work in itself and may
be considered for performance as such. Rhythmically, the motets are complex due to constant
overlapping of phrases and oft-changing motifs.
These motets are excellent material for training
a chorus in singing independent vocal lines and
developing rhythmic security. They are also musically worthwhile.

Unacc.   g-g''

Lasso, Orlando di   Bank #21

"Hodie Apparuit"

SSA   Easy   1 min.

This is a relatively easy example of imitative
polyphony of sixteenth-century style for three
equal voices. The work presents no difficulties
of harmonic or rhythmic elements. A few short
melismas occur; however, they are diatonic and
set at a moderate tempo. The three vocal lines
are all quite interesting melodically, with the
short thematic material of a rising fourth followed by three descending notes appearing in
each voice, somewhat as a "motto" theme.
This work would provide a conductor of a less-
experienced choir or glee club an excellent op-
portunity to introduce his singers to polyphonic
style within their performance abilities.

Unacc.   g-g''

ECS 1285, JF 6438

Lasso, Orlando di (ed. Paul Boepple)   Mercury DCS 21

"Three Psalms"
(on Texts and Tunes from Caspar Ulenberg's Psalter)

SSA   Diff.   1 min. each

1. Psalm 25, Judica Me Domine
2. Psalm 5, Verba Mea Auribus
3. Psalm 43, Veus, Auribus Nostris

These three psalms originally appeared in a collection of 53 psalms, half of which were by Lasso,
the other half by his son. Lasso has used Protestant tunes from Ulenberg's Psalter (1582) as
cantus firmi in these settings. All three of the
psalms are highly polyphonic in style, and some
of the diatonic scale passages are difficult to perform, mainly because of their rhythmic complexity.
Number two is perhaps the easiest, although all
three compositions make demands on alto range
and vocal control of all choir sections. This edition uses no bar lines, which helps proper text
accentuation but presents more difficult reading
problems to the amateur choir.

Unacc.   f-g"

Lawes, William (ed. WGW)   Ox JP 4

"Gather Your Rosebuds"
(adapted)

SSA   Med.   2-1/2 min.

This work is from John Playford's Musical Com-
panion, first published in 1667. It was used originally by a London musical club of which Playford
was a member. This work, with its famous text
by Herrick, is very much in the homophonic style
of the early seventeenth century. The work contains an occasional shift of meter to accommodate
the text, and crossing of the two highest voices
appears throughout, though resulting in no problems
of performance.

Unacc.   a^b-f"

Lawes, William (ed. WGW)   Ox JP xll

"Come Lovely Chloris"

SSA   Med.   2-1/2 min.

This work is clearly homophonic and illustrates
the musical style changes which were taking place
at the beginning of the seventeenth century. The

vocal parts are not difficult and the work is firmly tonal. There is some crossing of voices which
involves the second soprano part in the higher
register, but otherwise no problems occur as a
result of the crossing of such parts. The text is
very good and typical of the love ballads so popular during this period. A rehearsal piano part is
given, but in all likelihood the work was performed originally with harpsichord continuo.

Unacc.

g-a''

Lawes, William (ed. WGW)   Ox JP X1

"O My Clarissa"

SSA   Easy   2 min.

The tempo marking of Allegretto keeps this piece
in a light vein, although certainly the text, typical
of the English love ballads, is serious. Voice
crossings occur, but they do not create any performing problems. This work is easier than most
others in the Playford Collection. The use of the
minor key involves the lowered sixth degree contrasted with the raised seventh degree, but this
should present no problems.

Unacc.

g-g''

Liszt, Franz   GS 4392

"O Filli et Filiae"
(Easter Hymn)
(from Oratorio Christus)

SAA   Easy   2 min.

This is a simple setting of the popular "O Filii"
text, which has been set by a number of composers. The work is based on a modal melody
(Dorian mode) and therein lies its charm. This
setting, as are most settings of this text, is in
strophic form. Each subsequent verse employs
the same melodic material, with an Alleluia "refrain" preceding the work and closing it. The accompaniment is for Harmonium, a small reed type
instrument which was popular in the nineteenth
century, but a regular organ could undoubtedly
serve as a substitute. The accompaniment does
little more than double the voice parts (except in
the final cadence in which it has sole responsibility for establishing the terce di picardi chord)
and it could probably be excluded from a performance of the work.

Harmonium (or organ)

c'-c''

Liszt, Franz   BM

"The 137th Psalm"

SSAA (S)   Easy   12-15 min.

The text of this extended work by Liszt is one
which has attracted many composers. ("By the
rivers of Babylon, there we sat down, yea, we
wept".) The opening material of this cantata is
scored for soprano solo, violin obbligato and accompaniment in a style which the editors term
"mournful and mystical". The solo material is
not difficult in this section, nor in the sections
which follow. The remaining vocal material is
comprised of solo sections and choral sections
of long phrases which alternate on the word
"Jerusalem". The only text sung by the chorus
is the word "Jerusalem". This work is quite
simple and involves no technical demands on the
chorus singers except those associated with producing good tone quality and pitch accurateness
in soft passages.

Violin, harp, piano a^b-f"
and organ or Harmonium

Lotti, Antonio (ed. HC-L)   ECS 1845

"Mass" (in B^b)

SSA   Med.   30 min.

This mass, also available for men's voices, is
written in sixteenth-century polyphonic style, although composed in the early eighteenth century.
It is highly contrapuntal, and imitative counterpoint is common throughout. Part of the difficulty of this work rests on the fact that there is
a great deal of singing by all voice parts, with
practically no rests. Also, the soprano range
seems consistently high for an amateur group
and this could cause tiring and pitch-slipping.
Despite the emphasis on polyphony, the voice
parts are quite natural in their voice leadings
and melodic treatment. There are some excellent sections of falling suspensions, which can
be exquisite when sung sensitively.

Unacc.   g-g"

Lubeck, Vincent   Con 97-6379

"Christmas Cantata"

SS (or SA)   Easy   10 min.

This is an unpretentious, but expressive composition which has been fashioned most sensitively

in the Baroque Cantata tradition. An instrumental
sonata serves as an introduction to the vocal sections, which are comprised of three duets and
two solos, all rather brief. The instrumental accompaniment is employed throughout the composition, with the two violins scored in duet style and
often alternating passages with the vocal duet. This
cantata is not dramatic in the sense of contrasting tempos, rhythms or dynamics. Its dramatic
impact lies rather in the text, and the expressive
shadings and subtle beauties of the vocal lines in
combination with the instrumental accompaniment.
The range is simple, the vocal lines and harmonies are all diatonic, and even the instrumental
accompaniment is reasonably simple.

2 violins, cello (or bass)   f'-f''
and keyboard

Martini, Giambattista   SB 1824

"A Measure to Pleasure Your Leisure"
(with Rhymes That Are Witty and Pretty)

SSA   Med.   1-1/2 min.

This is a delightful glee of the early eighteenth
century. All the parts are great fun to sing and
the listener is sure to share in the jollity. The
voice parts are imitative in some places, but
for the most part the piece is scored as a duet
for soprano parts, with the alto line being complementary, but highly independent. There are
no difficult harmonic sections, nor are there
any difficult rhythmic sections. While the tempo
is marked fast, the text implies an occasional
change of tempo which adds some variety to the
work.

Unacc.   g-g''

Martini, Giambattista   Bank #24

"Tristes Est"

SSA   Easy-Med.   1 min.

This is a very simple, lovely motet in predominantly homophonic style. The work contains a
few brief passages which contain elements of
imitative counterpoint, but these are usually
scored as a single voice against two others
which are performing in duet style. The work
contains no difficult rhythm or harmonic elements. As in the case of a number of other
publications from this series (Bank), this would
be a good work for amateur choirs to perform

as an early experience in singing music of this period.

Unacc.   g-f''

Martinu, Bohuslav   Bo Ha 1945

"The Birth of Our Lord"
(Narozeni Pane)

SSA (divisi)   Med.   2 min.

A rather unusual setting of a unique text, this
work describes the circumstances of Christ's
birth in an original way. Each phrase length is
different in length. The vocal parts are fairly
rhythmic, with the violin part establishing an
almost "drone-like" effect, sometimes doubled
in one of the voices. Rhythmic and melodic patterns are often repeated in short phrases, both
in vocal lines and in the accompaniment. The
accompaniment eventually becomes independent
of the vocal parts and takes on a more melodic
role. A contrasting lyric-type section occurs in
the vocal parts prior to a repetitive ending. The
original Bohemian text is included with an English
translation by Nancy Bush.

Violin   b♭-g''

Mechem, Kirche   ECS 2561

"I Shall Not Care"

SSAA   Diff.   2 min.

This is a modern setting of a poem by Sara Teas-
dale. The composer has produced a fairly large
number of dissonant sounds through the use of
logical and melodic linear movement between the
voice parts. The work contains a variety of simple
rhythmic effects which prevent any monotonous use
of quarter note and half note patterns. Dynamic
contrasts are strategically placed to highlight the
text, although the work is not a dynamic or dramatic piece. This is an unpretentious composition, but one which contains many subleties and
nuances of expression. The rating of "difficult"
is assigned solely on the basis of the harmonic
effects created between voices; otherwise, it is a
work of only medium difficulty.

Unacc.   a-f#''

Mendelssohn, Felix   GS 5853

"I Would That My Love"

SS   Easy   3 min.

> This is a very lovely, simple two-part chorus
> written in duet style throughout. The style of
> composition is very much like that of the early
> romantic lieder, and the work contains a free
> flowing melody which is charming. The text, by
> the great German poet Heine, deals with roman-
> tic allusions to the subject of love. The range is
> reasonable and, except for an occasional chroma-
> tic linear progression, the work is quite diatonic
> and simple. Contrast is achieved in one small
> phrase section by scoring the voices in unison.
> Additional contrast is achieved in the piano ac-
> companiment, which, in typical romantic style,
> is very important to the overall effect. This is
> a work which can be handled easily by any choir
> with good results.

Accomp.   c#'-f#''

Mendelssohn, Felix   ECS 1839

"Ye Sons of Israel" (Op. 39 N. 2)
(Laudate Pueri)
SSA   Med.   4-1/2 min.

> This is a very stirring setting in paraphrase of
> Psalm 113:1, 2. The work is highly diatonic, not
> at all in the romantic style of the composer's
> day. The vocal parts contain a considerable de-
> gree of imitative devices; however, much of the
> work is homophonic in style. The accompaniment
> is designed chiefly to support the vocal parts, al-
> though it is quite florid. The work is quite fully
> scored throughout and tends to be rather power-
> ful, both as a result of the full scoring and the
> style of vocal writing. The vocal lines are not
> difficult and the intervals are all reasonable.

Organ or piano b^b-g''

Milhaud, Darius   Mercury MC 189

"Cantata From Proverbs"
SSA   Diff.   9-1/2 min.

> This work is divided into three sections as fol-
> lows:

1. Who Crieth "Woe"? (Proverbs XXIII:29-35)
2. The Woman Folly (Proverbs IX:13-18)
3. A Woman of Valor (Proverbs XXXI:10-31)

> They may be performed separately or as a group.
> Rhythmic syncopation is one of the chief charac-
> teristics of the work, and this feature gives the

work a high degree of vitality and interest. A
polyrhythmic treatment of the three vocal lines
is the result of the imitative treatment of the
text, although a homophonic-type text treatment
occurs frequently. The difficulty in this work may
be attributed to the melodic intervals employed.
They often result in modern-type chords, but the
harmonies are not essentially difficult or dissonant.
The accompaniment in each of the three sections
is independent and offers little harmonic or melodic
support to the vocal lines. Nevertheless, the effects
produced by the accompaniment are stunning and
contribute significantly to the overall effect of the
work. A keyboard instrument may be used if necessary.

Harp, oboe, cello   f#-a''

Miller, C. E.   GS 8515
            "Come Away, Sweet Love, and Play Thee"

SSA   Med.   2 min.

This is a delightful ballet madrigal by the eighteenth-century English composer, complete with "fa-
la" sections. It is scored with almost complete independence of parts, which shows that contrapuntal
writing certainly did not die out in the seventeenth
century. The vocal parts are not difficult, although
there is frequent crossing of vocal lines among all
voice parts. The contrapuntal style of the piece is
interrupted halfway through by a few brief homophonic sections, which alternate with polyphony.
This is an exceptionally effective madrigal.

Unacc.   b^b-g''

Miller, C. E.   Cur 71530
                    "I Saw Lovely Phyllis"

SSA   Med.   3 min.

This is another exceptionally good choral work by
Miller, but one which, judging by the text, has
been adapted for women's voices by the composer. Its composition style is considerably more
homophonic, with occasional phrases in unison.
The "fa-la" sections are more independent, in
the style of "Bach-type" resolving suspensions.
While the text is not well suited to women (the
words are obviously those of a young man), the
music is so charming that it hardly seems fair
to eliminate the song for this reason. A program
note explaining its musical worth and historic
stylistic significance would justify its use by a

women's choir.

Unacc.   a-f#''

<u>Miller, C. E.</u>   Cur 71512

"Welcome, Sweet Pleasure"

SSA   Med.   2 min.

> This is another excellent ballet madrigal by the
> little-known English composer, Miller. The work
> is basically homophonic, although there is con-
> siderable madrigal-type counterpoint throughout,
> especially in the "fa-la" refrain. The work has
> three verses, all set to the same music and each
> ending with the "fa-la" refrain. This is not a
> difficult work despite its counterpoint, and all the
> vocal lines are interesting to sing.

Unacc.   a-f#''

<u>Monteverdi, Claudio</u> (ed. Paul Boepple)   Mercury MC 24

"Sacrae Cantiunculae"
Nos. 12 & 16

SSA   Med.

> 1. Angelus Ad Pastores Ait   1 min.
> 2. Hodie Christus Natus Est   1-1/2 min.

> These two works, number 12 and number 16 of
> the 22 selections comprising the <u>Sacrae Canti-</u>
> <u>unculae,</u> were published when Monteverdi was
> only fifteen years old. Monteverdi, even at this
> early age, possessed a mature knowledge of the
> polyphonic style of his time. There are passages
> of imitative counterpoint included, but much of
> the counterpoint is less strict, yet no less im-
> pressive. Both of these works are for the Christ-
> mas season, but could be performed at any time
> using the Latin text. They present no major per-
> formance problems regarding rhythm or harmonic
> idiom and, compared with many works of this
> same period, are relatively easy, except for the
> overlapping of phrases. The first selection has
> two meter changes, from duple to triple meter
> and a return to duple meter.

Unacc.   f-g''

<u>Morley, Thomas</u>   ECS 283

"See! Lovely Day is Dawning"

SA   Med.   1-1/2 min.

This appears to be in its original form, in only

two voice parts. This work is not difficult, although as happens often with madrigals, there is
almost complete independence of parts. The work
contains a degree of imitation between the two
parts. There is a meter change partway through,
which affords a nice rhythmic contrast. The original common meter returns, before a final change
to triple meter at the conclusion.

Unacc.   b-e''

Nelson, Ron   Summy 5052

"Jehovah, Hear Our Prayer"

SSAA (S)   Med. Diff.   2-1/2 min.

Ron Nelson is a graduate of the Eastman School
of Music and served for some time as assistant
professor of music at Brown University and as
director of the Pembroke College Glee Club. The
text is based on selections from Psalms 13 and
22 and is a prayerful supplication to God. The
work begins with a chant-like melody sung in unaccompanied unison. The same material is also
used to close the work. In between, Nelson has
scored a finely wrought series of tonal prayers,
often in unisons, parallels, chant-effects and
contemporary progressions which achieve a stunning effect. Frequent changes of meter occur and
the work is enhanced further by an imaginative
accompaniment which is wholly independent. This
is an exceptionally fine and effective choral number and is not too difficult.

Piano   a-b#''

Palestrina, G. P.   GS 6251

"Ave Maria"

SSSA   Diff.   3 min.

This motet, based upon the familiar Gregorian
plain chant, is somewhat more complex than
many of Palestrina's works; however, it does
contain some sections which are paired off for
two or three voices in brief homophonic sections.
Imitation is an important basis of vocal line development and frequent chromatic alterations occur in the three lower parts. The first half of
the work contains the somewhat unusual feature
of the original Gregorian chant being stated in
the alto line, while above, the three soprano
parts weave a contrapuntal web out of the first
phrase of that chant, freely treated. The range
is fairly demanding of the three soprano parts.

>   This factor contributes to the difficulty of the
>   work.

Unacc.

a-f#''

Palestrina, G. P. (ed. GWW)   GS 9814

"Benedictus"
(from Mass O Admirabile Commercium)

SSA A   Med.-Diff.   3 min.

>   The mass O Admirabile Commercium takes its
>   name from the Christmas motet, and the com-
>   poser made two complete mass settings based
>   on the motet. (One for five voices, and one for
>   eight-part double chorus.) The "Benedictus" set-
>   ting is a somewhat slow-moving treatment of the
>   text and provides an excellent example of the
>   imitative, contrapuntal style and the "classical"
>   use of overlapping phrases. There are a few
>   short sections in homophonic style, but the major-
>   ity of the work treats the voice parts in an inde-
>   pendent, though interdependent manner. The dis-
>   sonances created by suspensions are typical of
>   sixteenth-century style, and the long, luring
>   melodic lines in each of the four voice parts
>   are largely diatonic, thus creating no modal
>   change problems. There are no complexities in
>   either rhythm or harmony. The work is a tradi-
>   tional presentation of polyphonic inter-weaving
>   texture.

Unacc.

f-g''

Palestrina, G. P.   GS 258

"Crucifixus"
(from Mass Assumpta est Maria)

SSA   Med.   1-1/2 min.

>   This excellent setting is a fine example of the
>   sixteenth-century polyphonic style of vocal writ-
>   ing. The vocal parts are often paired off in al-
>   ternating sections; however, a third voice is
>   usually employed contrapuntally in such sections.
>   There is a sufficient degree of homophonic sec-
>   tions which testify to Palestrina's more conser-
>   vative nature. Imitation, especially at points of
>   voice entries, is quite common and overlapping
>   of phrases, traditional in sixteenth-century poly-
>   phonic style, is commonly featured. The work
>   is highly diatonic, with no modal shifts employed,
>   although temporary modulations to the key of the
>   supertonic do occur.

Unacc.   g-f''

Palestrina, G. P.   GS 5605

"Innocentes pro Christo"

SSAA   Diff.   2-1/2 min.

This motet by Palestrina is polyphonic throughout, and the complete independence of vocal
lines, based heavily upon imitation, serves well
to dispel the notion that Palestrina was lacking
in the mastery of polyphony compared to his contemporaries. The work offers no evidence what-
soever of Palestrina's so-called conservatism,
but rather is highly complex and difficult. The
work is fully scored throughout, and heavy demand is placed upon the singers both in regard
to constancy in singing and the extremes of range
which treat the three upper parts equally. This
should be considered a work for SSSA, not SSAA.
Rhythm, intervals and melodic flow are all treated with complexity and will present problems to
all but the most advanced choirs; it is an exciting example of its style and period.

Unacc.

Palestrina, G. P. (ed. P. Boepple)   Mercury MC 12

"Magnificat"
(in the Fourth Mode)

SSAA   Med. Diff.   7 min.

This work is an excellent example of the Palestrina genius for contrapuntal writing. The
twelve text sections are scored alternately between a solo voice singing the plainsong (Gregorian chant) and the choral sections of imitative
counterpoint. The edition, like all the Mercury
publications under Paul Boepple's editorship, is
quite readable for amateur groups. The fourth
mode, in which this work is scored, may present some tonality problems to amateur singers
at first; however, no other major tonality problems
exist. The system of un-measured bar lines (except between staves for visual help) seems to be a
logical compromise to achieving textual fluidity.
Two of the six choral sections are scored only
for SSA, and the last section is more homophonic
than the others, although counterpoint is still employed.

Unacc.   a-f''

Peerson, Martin (ed. Peter Warlock)   Ox 339

"Cuckoo"

SS   Easy   1 min.

This is a simple madrigal-type work, for two
equal voices, which is scored for vocal lines of
a highly independent nature. Nevertheless the
composition is not difficult. The echoing of the
two vocal parts is charming and the number of
sections are scored in duet style. Peerson became master of the choristers and organist at
St. Paul's Cathedral and was a composer of instrumental and sacred choral music as well as
secular works. The original accompaniment is
for strings in three parts, but the piano accompaniment given is suitable for performance. The
vocal lines are highly diatonic and offer no real
rhythmic or harmonic problems. Dynamic variations are abundant throughout.

Accomp.   c'-f''

Peerson, Martin (ed. Peter Warlock)   Ox 339

"Come Pretty Wag"

SS   Easy   1 min.

This work is very easy, yet very delightful,
and in modified madrigal-style. The voice parts
are highly independent, although they occasionally join for duet sections which remain simple,
yet effective. The original accompaniment is
for strings in three parts, but the piano accompaniment supplied is suitable. While the melodic
and harmonic sections of this work are quite
simple, the rhythmic syncopation may necessi-
tate some special attention during first readings
of the work.

Piano   e'-e''

Pergolesi, Giovanni   P 5363

"Stabat Mater"

SA (SA)   Med.   46 min.

This work by Pergolesi is one of the most famous
extended works for women's voices, and deserving-
ly so. The duet and chorus sections contain some
of the finest two-part writing (duet style) in the entire repertoire. In these sections can be found
counterpoint, parallel movement, dissonances, suspensions and imitative writing, all skillfully treated. The solos are lyrical, rhythmic, expressive
and sensitively constructed in every instance. In
addition, the accompaniment, which is often

independent material, is an important part of the
entire structure. The work depends heavily upon
this accompaniment for its overall effect. This
selection is most effective in performance, especially so to the performers. It is certainly within
the ability level of high school groups as well as
those of the collegiate level.

String orchestra (or organ or piano)   c'-g''

GS, Kalmus, Ox. R 45422

Peters, Flor   De Ring, Antwerp

"Quatuor Motetta" (Op. 14)

SSA   Diff.   approx. 2 min. each

1. O Salutaris Hostia
2. Ave Maria
3. Vitam Petit a te
4. Tantum Ergo

These four motets are a welcome addition to
sacred Latin literature (of short length) in the
contemporary idiom. All except the fourth feature considerable independence of parts. However, each is characterized by a substantial
amount of parallel movement, resulting in some
degree of homophony and medieval flavor. There
are a number of interesting points of dissonance
throughout and the first three of the motets contain sections of brief imitative lines. The best
of the four is number three ("Vitam"), if only
because of its greater sense of unity and harmonic conception. The accompaniments, for the
most part, support the vocal material.

Organ   a-g''

Pfautsch, Lloyd   Flammer 89204

"Fanfare for Christmas"

SSAA   Med.   1 min.

This brief, jubilant fanfare is a welcome addition to the repertoire for women's voices. It is
an excellent opening selection for a Christmas
program. Practically all other existing fanfares
for similar purposes are for mixed voices. The
work must be performed with two trumpets and
two trombones as originally scored. With this
accompaniment, the work gains majestic excitement, as the voices alternate brief passages
with the instruments in a semi-Gabrieli style.
The vocal lines are quite rhythmic, as the composer employs brief elements of syncopation. The

harmonies are not difficult, and those of the instruments are usually repeated from, or in
sequence to, those of the vocal lines.

2 Trumpets and 2 trombones   a-a"

Pinkham, Daniel   ECS 2586

"If Ye Love Me"

SSA   Med.   2 min.

This is a relatively easy composition by Pinkham,
whose works are often beyond the performing level
of amateur choirs. The work contains frequent
shifts of meter, but if the text is carefully studied
for normal accentuations, the meter shifts should
present no major difficulties. The accompaniment
is also simply scored and complements the choral
setting of the text. The accompaniment often dupli-
cates the choral harmonies, and in this way supports the vocal sections. There are three unison
passages in the work which provide a refreshing
contrast to the harmonic scoring. The choral progressions are not difficult, yet provide some modern
sounds throughout the work.

Organ   b-f#"

Pinkham, Daniel   ECS 2572

"Three Lenten Poems of Richard Crashaw"

SSA   Diff.   5 min.

I. On the Still Surviving Marks of Our Savior's Wounds

II. Upon the Body of Our Blessed Lord, Naked
    and Bloody

III. O Save Us Then

This work was commissioned by the Wheelock College (Boston) Alumnae Association and Glee Club.
The work is difficult, mainly because of the in-
tense dissonance throughout. The second composition is scored for unison chorus; however, the
dissonances are still prevalent between the chorus
line and the accompaniment. The work presents no
rhythmic difficulties whatever, and although there
are frequent shifts of meter, they are not difficult
to negotiate, even for a true amateur choir. The
first two selections of the group are rather placid
and in a sostenuto style, the main emphasis being
directed to melodic interest. The third selection
is more dramatic in effect and provides a marked
contrast to the first two pieces. The harmonic
elements also receive more emphasis in this third

selection, and the dissonances are more poignant.

Str. Quartet (or str. orch.)   b-g"
and Handbells (or clesta or harp)
or keyboard accomp.

Poulenc, Francis

"Litanies"
a la Vierge Noire

SSA   Med.   8-10 min.

1. The Good Little Girl
2. The Lost Dog
3. When Coming Home from School
4. The Little Sick Dog
5. The Hedgehog

This work by Poulenc is filled with a great deal
of parallel voice movement, often based on chant-
like melodies. Frequent changes of meter lend
great interest and variety to the work, and a few
syncopated phrase beginnings offer additional rhythmic variety. While the vocal parts are relatively
reasonable throughout most of the work, there are
some sections near the end which contain difficult
intervals, especially in the second soprano part,
and some of the harmonies are of a more dissonant nature than the preceding sections. The typical
French idiomatic composition style is well represented in this work, and its effect is highly musical. If necessary, each selection could be performed separately.

Orchestra or organ   g-a"

Scarlatti, Alessandro   Ric NY 1894

"Stabat Mater"

SA (SA)   Med.   35 min.

Though overshadowed by the better known Pergolesi work of the same title, this setting of the
well-known "Stabat Mater" text by Scarlatti is de-
serving of more attention than has been accorded
it in recent years. The form of the composition
is very much like that of the Pergolesi work. It
is comprised of a series of solos and choruses,
with one duet included. The solo sections far out-
number the choruses; two of them (both for con-
tralto) are actually recitatives, an obvious musical vehicle for a composer of predominantly
operatic fame. The style of the "Stabat Mater"
is essentially that of a series of solos and duets
with basso continuo accompaniment. Scarlatti employs a large amount of chromaticism in this work,

both in the vocal lines and in the accompaniment. From a harmonic standpoint, the work
seems advanced for its time. While the chorus
sections in this work are relatively easy, the
solo sections are far more difficult.

Strings and piano (or organ)   g-g'' (chorus parts)

Schubert, Franz   Mercury MC 15

"Serenade"
"Ständchen" (Op. 135)

SSAA (A)   Diff.   5-1/2 min.

This work was composed by Schubert at the request of his friend Anna Froehlich in 1827. It
includes a very extensive and important alto solo,
which, while not technically demanding, is the
"heart" of the composition. In fact, this work
might be categorized as an alto solo with chorus
accompaniment. In addition to all of the vocal
material, the work is also scored for full piano
accompaniment throughout. Though the choral
parts are not melodically difficult, Schubert has
scored them in such a way that only the choir
with good vocal control should attempt to perform
this work. Many subtle and difficult dynamic shadings are included in these vocal lines and produce
technical challenges which must be considered.

Piano   g-b^{b}''

N. Trios 16

Schubert, Franz (ed. Max Spicker)   GS 9110

"The Lord Is My Shepherd"
(Gott meine Zunersicht)
(Psalm 23)

SSAA   Med.   8 min.

There seems to be considerable difficulty in finding good women's literature from the nineteenth
century, but surely this work by Schubert contains many stylistic features common to that
period. The work is in a homophonic style throughout, and features large amounts of chromatically
moving harmonies which are characteristic of early
Romantic music. The tempo indication by Schubert
is slow, the accompaniment is scored in arpeggiated triplet figures, and numerous passages are
carefully marked for crescendi and diminuendi; all
of these features contribute to a typically Romantic
setting of this famous Psalm text. A number of
brief passages are set in duet style between the two

upper or two lower parts, but the majority of the
work is in full four-part harmony.

Piano or organ   a^b-a$^{b''}$

N. Trios 67, O1-Dit 3196

Schumann, R.   N 166

"The Steadfast Heavens"

(Op. 144 N. 3)
SSS   Med.   2 min.

This work, the third in a group of three compositions in Schumann's Op. 114, appears to have a
better text than the others. The work is scored
in such a way that each voice takes up the original
melody while a second, and then a third, harmony
part is added to each successive presentation of
the melodic material. The vocal parts are not difficult and the work benefits greatly from the fine
piano accompaniment. Despite the seeming three
verses, or three presentations of the same melodic
material, the text is the same for all three. The
work ends with a three-part treatment of the text
which is effectively accompanied by the piano.

Piano   a-g''

Schuman, William   GS 8481

"Prelude for Women's Voices"

SSAA (S)   Diff.   6 min.

This work, composed in 1939 when the composer
was the conductor of the Sarah Lawrence College
Chorus, is a stirring and very exciting composition. The text by Thomas Wolfe lends itself well
to a choral setting of this type. While there are
numerous phrases of chromatic voice leadings
(all handled logically and thoughtfully by the composer), the work is still largely diatonic and much
of it is homophonic, with no polyphony used. The
lyric soprano solo is a most effective addition,
beneath which the vocal parts are scored in supportive harmony. A good soloist with a fine sense
of intonation and rhythmic security is essential to
the desired free-flowing effect, although the solo
itself is not difficult. Changes of meter signature
and tempo are present, but pose no difficulties.
Two unusual sections of the work are one in which
the chorus whispers rhythmically beneath the soloist and another at the ending in which the altos
sing 19 measures of pedal point "d" beneath the
closing phrases of the soloist.

Piano g-g''

Schuman, William GS 8928

"Requiescat"

SSAA Diff. 2 min.

This work, composed in 1942 for the Sarah Lawrence College Chorus and later arranged for
mixed voices, is a rather unusual and difficult
number. The two-part counterpoint is quite misleading, for its visual simplicity is betrayed by
rather difficult intervals and difficult dissonances
which include augmented ninths, diminished fourths
and minor seconds. The work is very effective,
both in its contrapuntal vocal lines and its rich,
full accompaniment. There is no text; the chorus
is directed only to hum throughout. The work employs an alternating meter shift between 4/4 and
3/4 for the first six measures and then settles
down to a 4/4 meter for the rest of its length.
The accompaniment is abandoned near the end,
with the final twelve measures sung mostly in
two-part counterpoint. The final two chords are
scored in four-part harmony.

Piano a^b-e''

Schütz, H. (ed. C. Buell Agey) Brodt WC 1

(Kleine geistliche Konzerte Bk. 1 No. 9)

"Blessed Is He Who Walks Not in the Paths of Godlessness"
(Wohl dem, der nicht wandelt im Rath der Gottlosen)

SA Med. 2-1/2 min.

This work is very similar in style to the other
two-part compositions from Schütz' Kleine geistliche
Konzerte collection. The manner of scoring the
vocal material is that of presenting the melody one
phrase at a time, with the second voice repeating
the preceding phrase at a different pitch level. Occasionally, an entire phrase is presented prior to
its repetition at another pitch, but often the repetition begins before the preceding presentation has
been completed. This results in excellent two-part
contrapuntal writing. The work is diatonic and employs no difficult harmonic or rhythmic elements.
Schütz does include several changes of tempo and
meter, which provide variety and contrasts within
the work.

Organ a-g''

Schütz, H. (ed. P. Boepple) MP MC 17

"Great Is Our Lord"
(Der Herr ist Gross)

SS   Med.   2-1/2 min.

This is one of several selections for equal voices
which are typical of Schütz' style. The chief characteristic of this work is essentially that of imitative counterpoint, which often presents the two
vocal lines in an alternating pattern of phrase presentation. The alternating pattern is occasionally
abandoned, however, giving way to a duet style.
The work is diatonic throughout, but many long
melismas occur in each of the vocal lines, which
accounts for the "medium" grade assignment listed in this annotation. This selection would be effective sung by solo voices, small chorus or a
larger group, provided the sections of the large
groups are balanced and capable of producing a
light and fluid sound.

Organ, harpsichord   c'f"
or piano (BC)

Schütz, H. (ed. C. Buell Agey)   Con 98-1558

"O Gracious Lord Our God"
(Sacred Concert Book I No. 6)

SS (2 equal)   Med.   3 min.

This duet begins with a twelve-measure phrase
by soprano I which is then repeated by soprano
II. The first soprano part joins this repeated
section and provides sections of both duet style
and canonic imitation. Following three coda-
like measures to the first section, the meter
switches from duple to triple for sixteen measures of canonic writing, which serves as a
second section to the composition. Following a
brief return to the style of the opening section,
the music then returns to triple meter for a
longer section of canonic imitation which also
employs some small amounts of seventeenth-
century duet-style writing. The vocal parts are
not particularly difficult; however, there are a
few minor shifts of modality which may cause
some pitch inaccuracies during early readings.

Organ   c'-f"

Schütz, H. (ed. William Herrmann)   Con 98-1414

"Sing O Ye Saints"
(Ihr Heiligen, Lobsinget dem Herren)

SS or SA (2 equal)   Med.   3 min.

This is another duet from the <u>Kleine</u> geistliche <u>Konzerte</u> collection. Much of the two-part writing occurs as alternating phrase patterns between the two voices, often based upon imitative melodic patterns. The work is not difficult in either its harmonic or melodic elements, but the rhythm of many of the melismas is difficult to articulate with full sections of sopranos (or sopranos and altos). There are a number of modal "shifts" occurring in the melodic material which need careful attention, and these, combined with the long melismas and the rhythmic problems, make the work more of a challenge than appears from a simple perusal of the score.

Organ   a-e"

Shaw, Martin   Cur 71470

"Sylvia Sleeps"
(No. 3 of <u>Four</u> <u>Pastorals</u>)

SA   Easy   1-1/2 min.

This is a simple setting in two parts, with arpeggiated piano accompaniment. The harmonic progressions are rather interesting, as the composer employs a modal-type shift between e minor (with its f# leading tone) and f major, with its b^b subdominant chord. Another interesting feature is the phrase structure, which is comprised of a five-measure phrase followed by a six-measure phrase. Following a two-measure piano interlude, this same pattern is repeated in a second verse. The work closes with an augmentation of the first two-measure pattern. The accompaniment, while quite simple, is very important to the effectiveness of this number.

Piano   g-f"

Shaw, Martin   GS 10041
                                                                       (Curwen catalog)

"With a Voice of Singing"

SSA (divisi)   Med.   2-1/2 min.

This is the well-known Anthem, originally scored for mixed voices, which the composer successfully rescored for women's voices. The work is highly spirited and energetic in its effect. Essentially, it is homophonic in style, although imitative entrances occur in several places, and the "pyramiding" effect of the "Alleluias" implies strong independence of vocal lines. Occasional phrases scored in unison lend excellent contrast

to the otherwise fully-scored sections. The predominantly independent organ accompaniment,
which is used to good effect, also provides interesting variety throughout the work.

Organ   f#-g"

Smith, Dorothy   Ox 582

"No Rose of Such Vertu"

SSAA (divisi)   Diff.   3 min.

This popular text has been set again with success
in this composition by Smith. Employing frequent
modulations and meter changes, the work conveys
an almost mystical effect to the listener. The
first verse is scored in a modern homophonic
style, sung by the three lower voices. The second
verse is given over to a first soprano solo, while
the three lower voices hum some unusual chordal
progressions. The verse continues in an alternating
pattern between the soprano voice and the lower
three voices. The third verse returns to the pattern of the first, but with a first soprano descant
line being added partway through. The final verse
returns to the style of the first, being sung only
by the three lower voices, beginning with the opening melody in a semi-cyclic form.

Unacc.   g-a$^\text{b}$"

Smith, Melville   W 3W2722

"Lully, Lullay"

SSAA   Med. -Diff.   2-1/2 min.

This is an unusually lovely and tender melody set
with both contrapuntal (non-imitative) and chordal
vocal support. Frequent meter changes, while
adding to the difficulty of the work, nevertheless
enhance the text accents considerably. The work
contains some fairly unusual progressions of
chords, but no difficult chords. The chords are
not dissonant in any modern sense, yet the work
has a distinctively modern sound. The anonymous
text is effective and the composer treats the contrasting sections appropriately, ranging from lyrical flowing phrases to the more marcato type,
to portray the sinister role of Herod. Following
these contrasts, the work returns to the tender
flow of the opening section.

Unacc.   f-g"

Stanford, C. V. (ed. WGW)   Ox 108

"Vitue"

SA   Easy   3 min.

> This is an exceptionally fine two-part work,
> completely through-composed. The accompani-
> ment is quite independent. The work is not dif-
> ficult, yet the effect is that of some degree of
> complexity. The two voice parts are often in-
> dependent, yet combine in many sections in
> duet style. The text by G. Herbert is artistic,
> despite the misleading title. The accompaniment,
> which is very effective, often employs a two-
> note descending "motive" which the voice parts
> also occasionally take up. This is a selection
> which is surely worthy of the attention of con-
> ductors whose choirs cannot handle more com-
> plex and difficult writing. The effect is that of
> high quality and workmanship, but the work is
> without the technical demands so often associated
> with such selections.

Piano   d'-g"

Thompson, Randall   ECS 2539

"Come In"
(from Frostiana)

SSA (divisi)   Med.   4-1/2 min.

> Two of the seven selections of the Frostiana col-
> lection are for women's voices, the rest being
> for either male or mixed voices. "Come In",
> with text by Robert Frost, is the first of the wo-
> men's numbers. This work is totally homophonic
> in style, yet contains many challenging demands
> upon a chorus to produce the subtleties and shad-
> ings of contrasting nuances and dynamic variations.
> One of the most impressive elements of the com-
> position is the piano accompaniment, which has
> the responsibility of setting the mood for the en-
> tire performance. Only the most musically sensi-
> tive of accompanists should be entrusted to the
> role. The harmonies of the vocal lines are not
> difficult, but the chordal changes are effectively
> scored in a variation between simple consonance
> and simple dissonance.

Piano   g-g"

Thompson, Randall   ECS 1985

"Now I Lay Me Down to Sleep"

SSA   Easy   1-1/2 min.

This is a simple but effective contrapuntal setting
of the familiar child's prayer. It is based on imitative counterpoint which is uncomplicated in modal
harmony or poly-textual effects. It would serve as
an excellent introduction to contrapuntal style for
an amateur chorus with little or no previous experience in singing polyphonic music. It is musically worthwhile as well. There are no difficult
intervals or harmonic effects, yet independence of
vocal lines is stressed by means of imitative counterpoint.

Unacc.   g-g''

Thompson, Randall   ECS 492

"Pueri Hebraeorium"

SSAA-SSAA (Antiphonal)   Med.   2-1/2 min.

There are few original works for women's voices
in antiphonal style. This one is very effective in
performance, especially when the two choirs are
placed at opposite sides of the stage or church.
This is a "festival-type" selection in that many
of the passages are fully scored for eight parts,
with the voices spread over the full practical com-
pass of the choirs' tessitura. Brief echo-like passages produce a joyful interplay between choruses
and the dynamic contrasts add to the effectiveness
of this interplay. Several shifts between duple and
triple meter add excitement to the work, as does
the occasional shift of tonality. The work contains
some rhythmic complexities and some of the snyco-
pations used will present some problems of ensemble in early readings.

Unacc.   g-a''

Thompson, Randall   ECS 2684

"The Lord Is My Shepherd"

SSAA   Easy-Med.   9 min.

This is Randall Thompson's most recent work for
women's voices. The style is often that which has
identified Thompson's music for years; however,
occasionally a chord progression or an accompaniment feature is new. The choral sections are
simply set, with long interludes by the accompaniment between sections of the text. The work contains several modulations, but each is presented
with adequate preparation in the accompaniment
before the vocal entrances. Only one change of
meter is introduced, and that is from 12/8 to
4/4, using the same four pulses per measure.

This selection exhibits considerable dynamic contrasts, but few tempo changes other than <u>rallen-
tandos</u> and normal returns to <u>a</u> <u>tempo</u>.

Piano, organ or harp   f#-a"

Vaughn-Williams, Ralph   Cur 71571

"It Was a Lover and His Lass"

SS   Diff.   2 min.

This text by Shakespeare has had many choral
settings, but none as fresh and interesting as
this one by the deceased "dean" of English contemporary music. While the setting is for only
two equal voices, it is nevertheless a fine work.
Its difficulty lies in the shifting of vocal parts between major and minor and also in a modal shift
within the melodic and harmonic passages caused
by the use of d natural in both E Major and E minor.
The work also contains an occasional change of
meter from 2/2 to 3/2, but this is not difficult.
The accompaniment is both interesting and varied
in style and lends considerable variety to the work.
While this may be a difficult selection to learn,
it is well worth the effort.

Piano   b-f#"

Vaughn-Williams, Ralph   Ox

"Lullaby"
(from the Cantata <u>This</u> <u>Day</u>)

SSA   Med.   3 min.

As in many of Vaughn-Williams' selections, this
work has a folk idiom "ring" to the melodic and
rhythmic style. It is a hauntingly lovely melody,
most often set in two-part harmony with a descant-
like part added. The "lullaby" text is interspersed
frequently between lines of Ballet's somewhat familiar text. A few relatively easy changes of time signature are artfully employed for the sake of the
text, and the entire selection is set in a minor key,
with a modulation to the subdominant key, and a
return to the tonic. The accompaniment is simply
scored, doubling the vocal lines and adding additional harmonic and melodic elements.

Piano   g-f"

Vaughn-Williams, Ralph   Ox 46-200

"Magnificat"

SSAA (A)   Med.   12 min.

The choral parts of this work are not at all difficult, even though modern sonorities are used occasionally. The alto solo, which comprises more
than half of the vocal portions, is quite difficult
and demands a very mature and sensitive soloist.
If orchestral parts (available from the publisher)
are not used, a skillful accompanist and flutist
are needed to perform this work. A large amount
of the choral sections is scored for unison chorus
and there are no difficult passages scored for chorus.
A number of key changes occur throughout the selection, but none involve the chorus. In general the work
is rather slow. While there are some dynamic contrasts indicated in the score, the tempos remain
slow throughout.

Orch. (or fl. and piano)   b-g'' (chorus)

Verdi, G.   P 4256c

"Laudi alla Vergine Maria"
(Hymn to the Virgin)
SSAA   Med.   5-1/2 min.

This selection is listed as number three in Verdi's
"Four Sacred Pieces". It is his only known work
for female choir. It is set in a solemn homophonic
style, although brief sections of independent part
writing are included. There are no meter or tempo
changes indicated, and the harmonies are not difficult to sing. Some demands are made upon the
soprano range, and there are long sostenuto phrases in all of the vocal parts. There are numerous
changes of dynamic markings indicated throughout,
although the majority of the work is placid and on
a soft dynamic level.

Unacc.   Ric 11457, AJB   f#-a''

Vullieinoz, Marguerite L.   Galaxy 999

"The Storke"

SSA   Easy   3 min.

This is a skillful setting of a lovely melody; the
text tells of the visit of the stork to the manger
in Bethlehem. The work begins with unison sopranos for the first verse. The second soprano
joins in on the second verse, and the alto part
is added to the third verse. The design is strophic.
The accompaniment is quite nice and varies considerably in the third verse. None of the vocal
parts are difficult and the voice leadings are carefully treated to insure ease of performance and
beauty of execution.

Piano or organ a^b-f"

Weelkes, Thomas   Kalmus 233
                            "A Country Paire"
SSA   Diff.   2-1/2 min.

This is a very difficult three-voice madrigal
which demands strict adherence to the rhythmic
syncopations. There is considerable independence
of vocal parts, although the top two soprano
parts are often treated in duet style. Imitation is
characteristic of the vocal treatment, as is the
use of suspensions, syncopations, and occasional
harmonic shifts from major to minor. The two
soprano parts are treated equally with regard to
range, as the second soprano involves the same
high register as the first. The alto part also presents range problems, as the alto line descends
to a low "f" in several places.

Unacc.   f-g"

Weelkes, Thomas (ed. EHF)   SB 1802
                     "Late in My Rash Accounting"
SSA   Med.   3 min.

This madrigal-style composition by Weelkes is
exceptionally well constructed. The tempo is not
too fast, and the "fa-la" refrain to each verse
is highly sequential between the two soprano
parts and the alto part. Melodically and harmonically, it demands complete independence among
the parts, although the two soprano parts are
treated in duet style almost completely throughout. A change of meter from 4/4 to 3/4 occurs
halfway through the second half, which invests
the work with some variety.

Unacc.   f-g"

Weelkes, Thomas (ed. EHF)   SB 1797
                   "The Gods Have Heard My Vows"
SSA   Med.   2 min.

This is a fairly simple example of sixteenth-
century madrigal-type composition, although
this work might more properly be classified as
an "air". The work contains an interesting combination of homophonic style combined with some
independence of vocal parts. There are three
verses contained in this selection, all set to the
same melodic and harmonic materials, each with
a short "fa-la" ending. There are no unusually

difficult harmonic or melodic sections, as the work
is essentially diatonic, especially in the melodic
lines of the three voice parts. The work does contain an unmarked shift of meter for a brief two
measures.

Unacc.   g-g"

Weelkes, Thomas (ed. EHF)   SB 1798

"Though My Carriage Be But Careless"

SSA   Med.   1-1/2 min.

This is another air from the "Collection of Airs
and Fantastic Spirits" by Weelkes catalogued under
Vol. 13. The text makes it particularly well suited
to women's voices. The work contains sufficient
chromatic alterations in the lower parts to cause
it to be a little difficult. The first half of the work
is largely homophonic in style; the second half involves independence of vocal parts. Near the end
of the work there is a fairly long pedal point in
the first soprano part, which is somewhat unusual
for a composition of this style period.

Unacc.   a-e"

Wilbye, John   SB M 6/2

"Away! Thou Shalt Not Love Me!"

SSA   Med.   2 min.

This is a fine madrigal by the important English
composer Wilbye. It is highly imitative in style,
with considerable independence of vocal lines.
Due to the rather brisk tempo and the almost
constant points of imitation, the use of modern
bar lines in this edition results in a fair degree
of complex rhythms throughout the work. This
produces a stirring melodic and rhythmic effect
throughout the madrigal. The chief melodic figure
employed is that of a descending scale pattern,
first in a pattern of eighth notes and then in a
dotted rhythm pattern in the second half of the
work. This is a very exciting number to perform,
and the counterpoint provides great interest.

Unacc.   g-g"

Wilbye, John (ed. EHF)   SB 1716

"Come Shepherd Swains"

SSA   Med.   2-1/2 min.

This work is an interesting mixture of homophonic

and contrapuntal style. While there are numerous
sections of vocal independence among the three
vocal parts, many phrases have the two soprano
parts in duet style, with an independent alto line.
Other phrase sections are highly homophonic in
the treatment of all three parts. Imitation is an
important composition element, although in this
selection it results in no rhythmic problems of
any consequence. The harmony is predominantly
diatonic, and the work presents no real performance difficulties, other than demands on extended
ranges both high and low.

Unacc.   f#-a"

Willan, Healey   BM 1808

"Oh! Queen of Heaven"
(Regina Coeli Letare)

SSAA   Med.   3 min.

This is a fine contemporary setting of the sixteenth-century text. While the vocal parts appear difficult, great care in the handling of voice leadings
and the frequent treatment of two parts as a unit
(altos against sopranos) actually result in a lessen-
ing of the apparent problems, so that the work is
not too complex or difficult. There are a few measures in which the vocal lines are independent; however, for the most part the work moves in extensive parallel design, both rhythmically and melodically. An occasional shift of time signature presents
no problems, and the text obviously benefits from
the resulting correct placing of accents. This is a
work which has been seriously neglected for no good
reason. The work is fully scored throughout, with
the full chorus singing most of the time.

Unacc.   gb-ab"

Williams, Catherine   GS 8446

"At Chrystemesse-Tyde"

SSAA   Diff.   2 min.

This is quite a different and unusual Christmas
selection, with a fine text by Willis Boyd Allen
("Two Sorrie Thyngs There Be"). The musical
setting is equally effective, although somewhat
difficult in sections. The voice leading is well
conceived, as the composer, anticipating vocal
difficulties of the average choir, has taken care
to score the vocal parts smoothly and logically.
In this regard, there are many sections in which
the two soprano parts are treated as a unit and
are contrasted with the unit of two alto parts.

This helps to make the work easier to perform,
as well as more structurally unified. The lack
of accompaniment puts more responsibility on
the singers, but the work certainly is in no need
of accompaniment either for harmonic or rhythmic
support, or as a means of providing variety.

Unacc.   f#-a''

Youll, Henry (ed. EHF)   SB 2475-20
                "Come, Merry Lads, Let Us Away"

SSA   Med.   1-1/2 min.

This is a merry canzonet of the English madrigal
school (early seventeenth century) by the little known
composer, Henry Youll. The work is both homophonic
and contrapuntal, containing a happy mixture of both
styles. The work is light and gay, and the voice parts
are relatively simple and uncomplex. Each vocal line
is treated in a diatonic fashion, and the resulting harmony offers no unusual key or modal changes. Even
the rhythm, which employs rhythmic and harmonic
suspension at cadence points, presents no problem in
execution. The work has a considerable degree of variety built into it, and the second half of the composition
employs considerable independence of vocal parts.

Unacc.   g-d''

Youll, Henry (ed EHF)   SB 2475-19
                "In the Merry Month of May"

SSA   Med.   2 min.

This is a delightful, fast moving canzonet, complete
with a "fa-la" section which is sheer delight to sing.
Considerable independence of voice parts is evident
throughout the work, but the vocal lines are so logically and melodically conceived that little or no
performance problems are apparent. Imitation is
predominant, and the "echoing" effect of the "fa-
la's" between the voices is both fresh and exciting.
Sequential patterns in the points of imitation are employed as a composition technique, but they are easy
to sing. Neither harmony, melody nor rhythm is a
problem anywhere within this work and, except for
an occasional low "g" in the alto part, the vocal
range is quite conservative.

Unacc.   g-e''

V. Recommended Arrangements

Aichinger, Gregor   Ric NY 1848

"Regina Coeli"
(Not the same composition as W 2900)

SSA   Ruggero Veni', arr.
(Unacc.)

Arcadelt, Jacob   ECS 1540

"Hear Thou My Prayer, O Lord"
("Ave Maria")

SSAA   Katherine K. Davis, arr.
(Unacc.)

Bach, J. S.   ECS 1051

"O Jesu So Sweet"
(O Jesulein süss)

SSAA   Katherine K. Davis, arr.
(Unacc.)

Barthelson, Joyce (Arr.)   LG 767

"Ding Dong, Merrily on High"

SSA   Joyce Barthelson, arr.
(Piano)

Bartholomew, M. (Arr.)   GS 9311

"Riddle Song"
("I Gave My Love a Cherry")

SSAA   M. Bartholomew, arr.
(Unacc.)

Bennet, John (Arr.)   Gray 512

"All Creatures Now Are Merry Minded"

SSA   John Bennet, arr.
(Unacc.)

Best, Jack (Arr.)   Shawnee Press B-158

"Three Highland Airs"

I Ae Fond Kiss
II Bonnie George Campbell
III Rest My Ain Bairnie

SSA   Jack Best, arr.
(Piano)

Bortniansky, D.   Gray 1000

"Cherubic Song"

SSA   Albert Ham, arr.
(Unacc.)

Brahms, J.   LG 51181

1. Down Low in the Valley
2. The Still of Night

SSA   Ivan Trusler, arr.
(Unacc.)

Brahms, J.   ECS 189

"Four Love Songs"

1. Was Once a Pretty, Tiny Birdie (Op. 52 N. 6)
2. In Wood Embowered, 'neath Azure Skies (Op. 52 N. 9)
3. No There Is No Bearing with These Spiteful Neighbors
                   (Op. 52 N. 11)
4. Secret Nook in Shady Spot (Op. 65 N. 8)

SSA   H. Clough-Leighter, arr.
(4-hand Piano)

Brahms, J.   ESV 855

"Magdalena"

SSAA   E. Harold Geer, arr.
(Unacc.)

Brahms, J.   ESV 896

"Praise of Mary"
(Marias Lob)

SSAA   E. Harold Geer, arr.
(Unacc.)

Brahms, J.   ESV 897

"Mary's Pilgrimage"
(Marias Wallfahrt)

SSAA
(Unacc.)   E. Harold Geer, arr.

Brahms, J.   ESV 886

"The Hunter"
(Der Jäger)

SSAA   E. Harold Greer, arr.
(Unacc.)

Brahms, J.   ECS 2505

"The Trysting Place" (Op. 31 N. 3)

(Der Gang Zum Liebehen)

SSA   Victoria Glaser, arr.
(Piano)

Brahms, J.   ECS 879

"Three Chorals from Motets Op. 29 N. 1 and Op. 74"

    1. To Us Salvation Now Is Come
    2. In Peace and Joy I Now Depart
    3. O Saviour, Open Heaven Wide

SSAA   E. Harold Geer, arr.
(Unacc.)

Brasart, Johannes   MP DCS 28

"O Flos Flagrans"
(A Song to the Blessed Virgin Mary)
(Note: correct title should be "O Flos Fragrans")

SSA   Paul Boepple, ed.
(Unacc.)

Burleigh, H. T. (Arr.)   Ric NY 693

"Were You There?"

SSA   H. T. Burleigh, arr.
(Unacc.)

Burt, Alfred   Shawnee Press B-161

"The Alfred Burt Carols"
(Set I)

    1. Caroling, Caroling
    2. All On a Christmas Morning
    3. We'll Dress the House
    4. Ah, Bleak and Chill the Wintry Wind

SSA   Hawley Ades, transcr.
(Unacc.)

Burt, Alfred   Shawnee Press B-160

"The Alfred Burt Carols"
(Set II)

    1. Oh Hearken Ye
    2. Some Children See Him
    3. Jesu Parvule
    4. Bright, Bright the Holly Berries
    5. The Star Carol

SSA   Hawley Ades, transcr.
(Unacc.)

Byrd, Wm.   SB 4873

"Cradle Song"

SSA   Edmund Horace Fellowes, arr.
(Piano)

Byrd, Wm.   ECS 815
"Sacerdotes Domini"

SSAA   G. Wallace Woodworth, arr.
(Unacc.)

Carissimi, G.   BM 11061
"O Felix Anima"

SSA   C. A. Garabedian, adapt.
(Unacc.)

Clarke, Douglas (Arr.)   BM 1838
"I Saw Three Ships Come Sailing In"

SSAA   Douglas Clarke, arr.
(Unacc.)

Collins, Leo (Arr.)   Row 6118

"Susanni"
(German Folk Song)

SSA   Leo Collins, arr.
(Unacc.)

Collins, Leo (Arr.)   Row 6117
"Mary's Lullaby"

SSA   Leo Collins, arr.
(Unacc.)

Collins, Leo (Arr.)   Row R6111
"The Rich Old Miser"

SSA   Leo Collins, arr.
(Piano)

Cope, Cecil (Arr.)   Bo Ha 1895
"Ten Christmas Carols"

(Intro.) Gloria in Excelsis Deo!
1. I Sing of a Maiden
2. What Is this Odour Round Us Flowing?
3. Wassail Song
4. Joseph, Joseph
5. A Babe Lies in the cradle
6. Quem Pastores
   (Shepherds Loud Their Praises Singing)

      7. In Dulci Jubilo
        (Good Christian Men Rejoice)
      8. The Holly and the Ivy
      9. The Angel Sang
    10. A Little Child There Is y-Born

SSA   Cecil Cope, arr.
(Unacc.)

Copland, Aaron (adapted)   Bo Ha 5025

         "Ching-A-Ring-Chaw"
           (Minstrel Song)

SSAA   Irving Fine, arr.
(Piano)

Copland, Aaron (adapted)   Bo Ha 1903

         "Simple Gifts"
          (Shaker Song)

SA   Irving Fine, arr.
(Piano)

Croce, Giovanni   01-Dit 14, 209

       "In Monte Oliveti"
    ("Upon the Mount of Olives")

SSA   Louis Victor Saar, arr.
(Unacc.)

Crueger, Johann   Con 18

    "Jesu, Priceless Treasure"

SSA   H. J. Markworth, setting & arr.
(Unacc.)

Cui, Cesar   ECS 1081

  "Radiant Stars, Above the Mountains Flowing"

SSAA   Katherine K. Davis, arr.
(Piano)

d'Astorga, Emmanuel   ECS 1983

     "Christe, quum sit jam exire"
 ("Christ, Now At Thy Passion" from Stabat Mater)

SSA   Victoria Glaser, arr.
(Organ)

Davison, Archibald T. (Arr.)   ECS 1513

       "Turn Ye to Me"

SSA   Archibald T. Davison, arr.
(Piano)

Davis, Katherine K. (Arr.)   Summy B-140
        "I Gave My Love a Pretty Little Ring"
SSA   Katherine K. Davis, arr.
(Piano)

Davis, Katherine K. (Arr.)   ECS 1058
        "Tween the Mount and Deep, Deep Vale"
SSA   Katherine K. Davis, arr.
(Piano)

Debussy, Claude   GS 5992
              "The Rain Falls on My Heart"
              ("Il Pleure dans Mon Coeur")
SSAA (divisi)   Jeanne Boyd, arr.
(Piano)

Des Préz, Josquin   ECS 816
                    "Ave Verum"
SSA   G. Wallace Woodworth, arr.
(Unacc.)

Dickinson, Clarence (Arr.)   Gray 259
            "Angels O'er the Fields"
SSAA
(Organ ad lib.)   Clarence Dickinson, arr.

Dowland, John   ECS 1085
        "Come Again! Sweet Love Doth Now Invite"
SSAA   Katherine K. Davis, arr.
(Unacc.)

Dowland, John   JF 7377

        "Say, Love, If Ever Thou Didst Find"
SSA   Gwynn S. Bement, arr.
(Unacc.)

Erb, James (Arr.)   LG 51036

                    "Medieval Triptych"

                I Gregorian Chant
               II Conductus (early 13th Century)
              III Motet (late 13th Century)
SSA   James Erb, arr.
(Percussion)

Ericksen, Frederick (Arr.)   Gray 1261
                          "Deck the Halls"
SSA   Frederick Ericksen, arr.
(Unacc.)

Frackenpohl, Arthur (Arr.)   Mills 683
                          "The Bird's Song"
SSA   Arthur Frackenpohl, arr.
(Piano)

Gasparini, Quirino   GS 8154
                          "Adoramus Te"
SSAA   Katherine K. Davis, arr.
(Unacc.)

Geer, E. Harold (Arr.)   ECS 822
                     "Ding Dong! Merrily on High"
SSAA   E. Harold Geer, arr.
(Unacc.)

Geer, E. Harold (Arr.)   ECS 1919
                     "Christ the Lord Hath Risen"
SSA   E. Harold Geer, arr.
(Unacc.)

Geer, E. Harold (Arr.)   ESV 898

                          "Noel Nouvelet"
                         (Sing a New Noel)
SSAA (S)   E. Harold Geer, arr.
(Unacc.)

Gevaert, Francois   W 3W 2858

                     "Joyous Christmas Song"
                    (Chanson Joyeuse de Noel)
SSAA   Max T. Krone, arr.
(Unacc.)

Gibbons, Orlando   ECS 1932
                     "O Lord, Increase My Faith"
SSAA   Arthur S. Talmadge, arr.
(Unacc.)

Gibbons, Orlando   SB 251
                          "The Silver Swan"
SSA   Edmund Horace Fellowes, adapt.

(Unacc.)

Glaser, Victoria (Arr.)   ECS 1959

"The Twelve Days of Christmas"

SSAA (S)   Victoria Glaser, arr.
(Piano)

Handl, Jacob   GS 8441

"Pueri Concinite"
("Children Come")

SSAA   E. Harold Geer, ed.
(Unacc.)

Hassler, Hans L.   ECS 1887

"Cantate Domino"
(O Sing unto The Lord)

SSAA   Gwynn S. Bement, arr.
(Unacc.)

Hassler, Hans L.   ECS 1918

"Crucifixus Etiam pro Nobis"
(from the Credo Mass I)

SA   Arthur S. Talmadge, ed. & arr.
(Unacc.)

Holst, Imogen (Arr.)   Ox 2470

"Six Traditional Carols"

1. The Holly and the Ivy
2. Joys Seven
3. A Virgin Most Pure
4. I Saw Three Ships
5. Bedfordshire Mayday Carol
6. Matthew, Mark and Luke and John

SSA   Imogen Holst, arr.
(Unacc.)

Isaac, Heinrich   ECS 1923

"My Only Joy in All the World"

SSAA   Victoria Glaser, arr.
(Unacc.)

Jacob, Gordon (Arr.)   Ox 558

"Brother James' Air"

SSA   Gordon Jacob, arr.
(Piano)

<u>Jonequin, Clement</u>   ECS 1987

"Ce Moys de May"
(This Month of May)

SSA   Alfred Finch, arr.
(Piano)

<u>Jungst, Hugo</u> (Arr.)   Gray

"While Shepherds Watched Their Sheep"

SSAA   Hugo Jungst, arr.
(Unacc.)

<u>Kent, Richard</u> (Arr.)   LG 51216

"Fare Thee Well, O Honey"

SSA   Richard Kent, arr.
(Unacc.)

<u>Kodaly, Z.</u> (Arr.)   Ox 503

"See the Gipsy"

SSAA   Z. Kodaly, arr.
(Unacc.)

<u>Kodaly, Z.</u> (Arr.)   Ox 502

"The Straw Guy"

SSAA   Z. Kodaly, arr.
(Unacc.)

<u>Kubik, Gail</u>   Southern

"Little Bird, Little Bird"

SSSSAAAA   John Klein, arr.
(Piano)

<u>Kubik, Gail</u> (Arr.)   GS 9995

"Oh Dear! What Can the Matter Be?"

SSA (divisi)   Gail Kubik, arr.
(Unacc.)

<u>Lasso, Orlando di</u>   ECS 1811

"Echo Song"

SSA-SSA   Elizabeth Marting, arr.
(Unacc.)

<u>Lasso, Orlando di</u>   01-Dit 332-13101

"Matona, Lovely Maiden"

SSA   Louis Victor Saar,   arr.

(Unacc.)

Lathrop, Roy (Arr.)   Pro-Art 1020

"Whistle and I'll Come to You"
(Scotch Tune)

SSA   Roy Lathrop, arr.
(Piano)

Leontovich, M.   CF CM 5276

"Carol of the Bells"

SSA   Peter Wilhousky, arr.
(Unacc.)

Lotti, Antonio   ECS 1949

"Agnus Dei"
(Lamb of God)
(from Mass VII)

SSAA   Arthur S. Talmadge, arr.
(Unacc.)

Lotti, Antonio   ECS 1904

"Kyrie"
(from Mass VII)

SSAA   Arthur S. Talmadge, arr.
(Unacc.)

Lotti, Antonio   Remick 3-G 1541

"Regina Coeli"
(Queen of the Heavens)

SSAA
(Unacc.)   Don Malin, arr.

Lotti, Antonio   ECS 1509

"Vere Languores Nostros"
(Surely He Hath Borne Our Grief)

SSA   G. Wallace Woodworth, arr.
(Unacc.)

Lvovsky, S. V.   HWG 1536

"Hospodi Pomilui"

SSAA   Boris Levenson, transcr.
(Unacc.)

Menegali, Martin Joseph   BM 11421

"Ave Regina"

SSA   C. A. Garabedian, adapt.
(Unacc.)

Mendelssohn, F.   GS 4371
    "How Lovely Are the Messengers"
      (from St. Paul)
SSA
(Piano)   Max Spicker, arr.

Morales, Cristobal de   GS 11077
     "O Magnum Mysterium"
SSAA   Robert Goudale, ed.
(Unacc.)

Morley, Thomas   GS 8156
    "April Is in My Mistress' Face"
SSAA   Katherine K. Davis, arr.
(Unacc.)

Morley, Thomas   JF 7415
    "Come Lovers, Follow Me"
SSA
(Unacc.)   Gwynn S. Bement, arr.

Morley, Thomas   Hall & McCr. 2068
    "Fire, Fire My Heart"
SSAA   Kenneth Runkel, arr.
(Unacc.)

Morley, Thomas   01-Dit 13568
    "It Was a Lover And His Lass"

SSAA   Arthur Fagge, arr.
(Unacc.)

Morley, Thomas   JF 7593
     "I Will No More"
    (from "Madrigalls to Foure Voyces")
SSAA   Gwynn S. Bement, arr.
(Unacc.)

Morley, Thomas   N 483
    "My Bonny Lass She Smileth"
SSAA   John West, arr.
(Unacc.)

Morley, Thomas   ECS 825

"Now Is the Month of Maying"

SSAA   G. Wallace Woodworth, arr.
(Unacc.)

Morley, Thomas   N 479

"What Saith My Dainty Darling"

SSAA   John West, arr.
(Unacc.)

Mueller, Carl F. (Arr.)   GS 8159

"Blow, Winds, O Softly Blow"

SSA   Carl F. Mueller, arr.
(Piano)

Niles, J. J. (Arr.)   GS 8305

"I Wonder As I Wander"

SSAA (S)   J. J. Niles, arr.
(Unacc.)

Niles, J. J. (Arr.)   GS 9479

"Never Was a Child So Lovely"

SSAA   J. J. Niles & Amand Parsons, arr.
(Unacc.)

Niles, John Jacob &   GS 11206
Sheppard, J. Stanley (Arrs.)

"The Lass from the Low Countree"

SSAA   John Jacob Niles &
(Piano)   J. Stanley Sheppard, arrs.

Nin, Joaquin (Transcr.)   AMP

"And the Angel Woke the Shepherds"
(No. 2 of Four Spanish Folk Songs)

SSAA
(Piano)   Joaquin Nin, transcr.

Palestrina, G. P.   ECS 1962

"Ascendit Deus"

SSAA   Kenneth Runkel, arr.
(Unacc.)

Palestrina, G. P.   JF 7302

"Benedictus"
(from Missa Brevis)

SSA   Gwynn S. Bement, ed.
(Unacc.)

Palestrina, G. P. (et. al.)   ESV 869
                        "Four Responses"

SSAA   1. Gloria Patri   (Palestrina)
SSA   2. Jesu Salvator Mundi   (Menegali)
SSA   3. Non, Nobis, Domine   (Byrd)
SSAA   4. Christus Factus Est   (Handl, J.)
(Unacc.)   E. Harold Geer, arr. & ed.

Palestrina, G. P.   JF 7422
              "My Heart It Seemed Was Dying"
                 (Mori Quasi il mio core)
SSAA   Gwynn S. Bement, arr.
(Unacc.)

Palestrina, G. P.   ECS 1812
                        "O Bone Jesu"

SSAA   H. Clough-Leighter, arr.
(Unacc.)

Parrish, Carl (setting)   W 2W 8236
                      "Oh Rise Shine!"

SSA   Carl Parrish, setting
(Unacc.)

Peerson, M.   Galaxy 1082
              "Upon My Lap My Soveraigne Sits"

SSAA   Katherine K. Davis, arr.
(Unacc.)

Praetorius, Michael   CF CM 411
                      "In Dulci Jubilo"

SA   E. Harold Geer, transcr.
(Unacc.)

Praetorius, Michael   ECS 1993
                    "In Natili Domini"
             (At the Sweet Birth of Our Lord)

SSA   Victoria Glaser, arr.
(Unacc.)

Purcell, H.   ECS 487
                    "Sound The Trumpet"
                    ("Welcome Song")

SA   Alfred Moffat, arr.
(Piano)

Riegger, Wallingford (Arr.)   Flammer 86048
                        "Beautiful Saviour"
                        (Crusader's Hymn)
SA (S)   Wallingford Riegger, arr.
(Piano or organ)

Roselli, F.   01-Dit 14, 206
                        "Adoramus Te"
SSA
(Unacc.)   Louis Victor Saar, arr.

Ryder, Wm. (Arr.)   Ric NY 728
                        "Drink to Me Only"
SSAA   Wm. Ryder, arr.
(Unacc.)

Schein, John H.   Row 498
        "Three Sacred Concerts for the Christmas Season"
                        I Now Come, the Heathen's Saviour
                        II All Praise Be Thine, Lord Jesus Christ
                        III From Heaven on High, I Come to You
SSA   Edward Low & Daniel Pinkham,   editors
(Organ)

Schubert, Franz   LG 789
                        "The Echo"
SSA   .   Wendell J. Rider, arr.
(Piano)

Schuman, Wm. (Arr.)   GS 8948
                        "Holiday Song"
SSA   Wendell J. Rider, arr.
(Piano)

Schuman, Wm. (Arr.)   GS 9212
                        "The Orchestra Song"
6 parts   Wm. Schuman, arr.
(any comb. of voices)
(Unacc.)
Schütz, H.   GS 8981
                        "Veni, Rogo, in Cor Meum"

(Come I Pray Thee, Dwell Within Me)

SSAA   E. Harold Geer, arr.
(Unacc.)

Spicker, Max (Arr.)   GS 439

"While by My Sheep"
("Christmas Hymn")

SSAA   Max Spicker, arr.
(Unacc.)

Stellhorn, A. W. (Arr.)   Con 5

"Let Us All with Gladsome Voice"

SSAA   A. W. Stellhorn, arr.
(Unacc.)

Sweelinck, Jan Pieters   BM 2361

"Or Sus, Serviteurs du Seigneur"
(Arise, All Ye Servants of the Lord)
Psalm CXXXIV

SSAA   Margaret Macdonald, arr.
(Unacc.)

Tallis, Thomas   C F CM 402

"Nunc Dimittis"
(from Evening Service in Dorian Mode)

SSAA (or double choir)   Arthur E. Egerton, arr.
(Unacc.)

Terri, Salli (Arr.)   LG 666

"Away in a Manger"

SSA   Salli Terri, arr.
(Opt. harp or piano)

Thiman, Eric H. (Arr.)   Gray 2402

"O Brother Man"

SA (divisi)   Eric H. Thiman, arr.
(Piano)

Thompson, Virgil (Arr.)   Gray 2294

"My Shepherd Will Supply My Need"

SSAA   Virgil Thompson, arr.
(Unacc.)

Tschesnokoff, Paul   Bourne WE 7

"Salvation Is Created!"

SSA   Walter Ehret, arr.
(Unacc.)

Treharne, Bryceson (Setting)   BM 1901
                    "Child in the Manger"
SSA   Bryceson Treharne, setting
(Piano)

Treharne, Bryceson (Setting)   BM 1519
                        "Star Lullaby"
SA   Bryceson Treharne, setting
(Piano)

Treharne, Bryceson (Setting)   BM 1527
                      "The Elfin Horn"
SSA   Bryceson Treharne, setting
(Piano)

Vaughn-Williams (Arr.)   Ox
                "Folk Songs of the Four Seasons"
                            (Cantata)
SSA   Vaughn-Williams, arr.
(Orch. or piano)

Vecchi, Orazio   LG 741
                        "Sing Me a Song"
                        (Fa una Canzone)
SSAA   Jerry Weseley Harris, arr.
(Unacc.)

Vene', Ruggero (Arr.)   AMP
                    Six French Folk Songs

            1. Au Clair de la Lune   (AMP 96)
            2. Si le Roy M'avait Donne'   ("   97)
            3. Pavanne   ("   98)
            4. Les Trois Princesses   ("   99)
            5. En Passant par la Lorraine   (" 100)
            6. Jardin d'Amour   (" 101)
SSA   Ruggero Vene', arr.
(Piano)

Vittoria, T. L. da   JF 5050
                        "Ave Maria"
SSAA   D. Taylor, arr.
(Unacc.)

Vittoria, T. L. da   01-Dit 13, 381

"Duo Seraphim"
("Lo, Two Seraphim")

SSAA   Kurt Schindler, ed.
(Unacc.)

Vittoria, T. L. da   ECS 1941

"Gaudent in Caelis"

SSAA   Arthur S. Talmadge, arr.
(Unacc.)

Vittoria, T. L. da   ECS 830

"Jesu, Dulcis Memoria"
(Jesus, the Very Thought of Thee)

SSAA   G. Wallace Woodworth, arr.
(Unacc.)

Vittoria, T. L. da   ECS 1922

"O Magnum Mysterium"

SSAA   Victoria Glaser, arr.
(Unacc.)

Vittoria, L. T. da   ESV 871

"O Vos Omnes"
(O Ye People)

SSAA   E. Harold Geer, ed.
(Unacc.)

Vittoria, T. L. da   ECS 1507

"Tanquam Agnus"

SSA   Archibald T. Davison, ed.
(Unacc.)

Vulpius, Melchoir   Gray 148

"An Easter Hallelujah"

SSAA-SSAA   E. Harold Geer, arr.
double chorus
(Unacc.)

Weelkes, T.   SB 252

"Sing We at Pleasure"

SSA   Edmund Horace Fellowes, adapt.
(Unacc.)

Weelkes, T.   01-Dit 15099

"Welcome Sweet Pleasure"

SSA   Gwynn S. Bement, arr.
(Unacc.)

West, John (Arr.)   N 222

"The Bonnie Banks of Loch Lomond"

SA   John West, arr.
(Piano)

Weston, Philip (Arr.)   Elkan

"Greensleeves"

SSAA   Philip Weston, arr.
(Piano)

Wilbye, John   ECS 1076

"Adieu, Sweet Amarillas"

SSAA   Katherine K. Davis, arr.
(Unacc.)

Williams, John Gerrard (Arr.)   Cur 71563

"Early One Morning"

SA   John Gerrard Williams, arr.
(Piano)

Zanzig, Augustus D. (Arr.)   ECS 1906

"Once Long Ago"

SSA   Augustus D. Zanzig,   arr.
(Piano)

Chapter V
Indices

The index lists in this chapter provide a series of cross references to the musical works listed and annotated in this study. The page number reference given after each title refers to a page in Chapter Four, where more complete information regarding that composition may be found.

A separate index for each of the following categories is provided: (1) titles of compositions alphabetically arranged, (2) number of vocal parts, (3) grade of difficulty (original works only), (4) compositions of extended length and (5) collections and their contents.

In the index of collections, works are cited under the heading of the collection title. Works so cited have not been annotated in Chapter Four, but they may be presumed to be of the same quality.

I. Index of Titles

Title	Composer	Page
Adieu, Sweet Amarillas	Wilbye-Davis	136
Adoramus	Brahms	64
Adoramus Te	Gasparini-Davis	125
Adoramus Te	Roselli-Saar	132
Adoramus Te	Lasso	88
Adoramus Te Christe (fr. Magnum Opus Musicum	Lasso	88
Ae Fond Kiss	Best (arr.)	119
Agnus Dei	Lotti-Talmadge	128
Ala Vierge Noire	Poulenc	104
Alfred Burt carols, The (Set I)	Burt-Ades	121
Alfred Burt carols, The (Set II)	Burt-Ades	121
All Creatures Now Are Merry Minded	Bennet (arr.)	119
And the Angel Woke the Shepherds	Nin (arr.)	130
Angelic Greeting, The	Brahms-Geer	120
Angels o'er the Fields	Dickinson (arr.)	124
Angelus ad pastores ait & Hodie Christus natus est (fr. Sacrae Cantiunculae)	Monteverdi	97

II. Index of Number of Parts

SA

SSA

III. Index of Grade of Difficulty

Easy

Medium

Difficult

IV. Index of Works of Extended Length

V. Index of Recommended Collections

A Cappella Singer, The. A Collection of Motets, Madrigals, Chansons, Carols, Ayres, Ballets, etc. Edited by H. Clough-Leighter. Boston: E. C. Schirmer Music Company, 1936.

Bortniansky   Lo, a Voice to Heaven Sounding
Brahms   Charm Me Asleep
Cui   Radiant Stars, about the Mountains

Art of Polyphonic Song, The. Compositions of the Sixteenth and Seventeenth Centuries for Two to Eight Parts. Edited by Hans David. New York: G. Schirmer, 1940.

Composer	Title
Weelkes	Come Sirrah Jack, ho
Weelkes	Ha ha, This World Doth Pass
Weelkes	Lo, Country Sports
Weelkes	The Nightingale, the Organ of Delight
Wilbye	As Fair as Morn

Carols for the Seasons. Settings by Healey Willan. St. Louis: Concordia Publishing House, 1959.

All My Heart Today Rejoices
Ascended Is Our God and Lord
Away in a Manger
Beautiful Savior
Child in the Manger
Come, Souls, Behold Today
From Heaven High I Come to Earth
Good Christian Men, Rejoice
He Whom Joyous Shepherds Praised
Lord's My Shepherd, The (Brother James' air)
Love Came Down at Christmas
Maria Walks amid the Thorn
Now Let the Heavens Be Joyful
Oh, Come, All Ye Faithful
Oh, How Beautiful the Sky
O Little Town of Bethlehem
Prepare the Way, O Zion
Shepherds Watched Their Flocks by Night
Sing to the Lord of Harvest
Spring Carol, A
This Joyful Eastertide
What Star is This, with Beams so Bright

Canzonets for Two Voices by Thomas Morley. Edited by Edmund H. Fellowes. London: Stainer and Bell.

Fire and Lightning from Heaven
Flora, Wilt Thou Torment Me?
Go Ye, My Cansonets
I Go Before, My Darling
In Nets of Golden Wires
I Should for Grief and Anguish
Leave Now, Mine Eyes
Lo, Here Another Love
Miraculous Love's Wounding
O Thou that Art So Cruel
Sweet Nymph, Come to Thy Lover
When Lo, by Break of Morning

Canzonettens. Eleven Canzonetts for Three Equal Voices by Claudio Monteverdi. Edited by Hilman Trede. Kassel: Bärenreiter.

Chi Vuol Veder un Bosco
Come Faro Cour Mio quando mi Parto
Corse a la Morte il
Gia Mi Credevim

Giu Lia quel Petto Giace
Godi pur del Bel Sen
Hor Care Canzonette
Io mi Vivea
Io Son Fenice
Si Come Crescon
Vita de l'Alura Mia

Eighteen Duets for Soprano and Alto from the Cantatas by Johann S.
Bach. English translated and edited by Henry S. Drinker. Philadelphia: University of Pennsylvania Choral Series.

Ach Herr, mein Gott, vergib mir's doch
Beruft Gott selbst, so muss der segen
Den tod niemand zwingen kunnt
Die armut, so Gott auf sich nimmt
Domine Deus, agnus Dei, (Latin only)
Entziehe dich eilends, mein herze, der welt
Er kennt die rechten freudenstunden
Gedenk an Jesu bittern tod
Herr, du siehst statt guter warke
Herr Gott Vaterm mein starker held
Herz, zerreiss des mammons kette
Ich folge dir nach
Ihr klaget mif seufzen, ich jauchze mit schall
Nimm mich mir und gib mich dir
Nun komm, der Heiden Heiland
Weichet, weichet, furcht und schrecken
Wenn des kreuzes bitterkeiten
Wir eilen mit schwachen, doch emsigen schritten

Laudate Pueri. Sacred Music of the Sixteenth Century. Edited by
Donald Tovey. London: Augener, 1910.

Composer	Title
Agostini	Adoramus Te
Constantini	Confitemini Domino
Croce	Et Resurrexit
Gabrieli	Crucifixus
Lasso	Adoramus Te
Lasso	Agimus Tibi Gratias
Lasso	Alleluja Laus et Gloria
Lasso	Benedictus Qui Venit
Lasso	Expandi Manus
Lasso	Hodie Apparuit in Israel
Lasso	Ipsa te Cogat Pietas
Lasso	In Pace in Idipsum Dormiam
Lasso	Oculus non Vidit
Lasso	Sancti Mei
Mozart	Alleluja
Mozart	Ave Maria
Mozart	Kyrie Eleison
Palestrina	Adoramus Te
Palestrina	Benedictus Qui Venit

Composer	Title
Palestrina	Benedictus Qui Venit
Palestrina	Confitemini Domino
Palestrina	Crucifixus
Palestrina	Hodie Christus Natus Est
Palestrina	Jesu Rex Admirabilis
Palestrina	Pleni sunt Coeli
Palestrina	Salve Regina
Palestrina	Tua Jesu Dilectio
Vittoria (Victoria, T. L.)	Accende Lumen Sensibus
Vittoria	Christe Eleison
Vittoria	Duo Seraphim
Vittoria	O Sacrum Convivium
Vittoria	O Vos Omnes

Madrigals for Treble Voices. Edited and arranged by Donald Malin. New York: The B. F. Wood Music Company, Inc., 1964.

de Wert	The Messenger of Love
Dowland	A Shepherd in a Shade
Gastoldi	Maidens Fair of Mantua's City
Gibbons	The Silver Swan
Lasso	My Heart to Thee Now Makes Its Plea
Morley	It Was a Lover and His Lass
Morley	Now Is the Month of Maying
Vecchi	Let All Who Sing Be Merry
Weelkes	Since Robin Hood
Weelkes	Some Men Desire Spouses
Weelkes	To Shorten Winter's Sadness

Mediaeval and Renaissance Choral Music for Equal Voices A Cappella. Edited by Georgia Stevens. Boston: Mc Laughlin and Reilly Company, 1940.

Animuccia	Kyrie
Anonymous	Alleluia-Angelus Domini
Anonymous	Alleluia Psallet
Anonymous	Hymn of St. Adalbert
Anonymous	Catalan Folk Songs
Anonymous	German Flagellants' Hymn
Anonymous	O Miranda Dei Garitas
Anonymous	Puellare Gremium
Anonymous	Sanctus
Dufay	Flos Florum
Dunstable	Quam Pulchra Es
Lasso	Benedictus
Leoninus	Haec Dies
Obrecht	Missa Sine Nomine
Obrecht	Qui cum Patre
Ott	Dies Est Laetitiae
Ott	On This Our Joyful Holiday
Palestrina	Pueri Hebraeorum
Tallis	Sancte Deus
Taverner	Audivi

Composer	Title
Taverner	Gloria in Excelsis
Vittoria	Judas Mercator
Vittoria	Una Hora

Morning Star Choir Book, The. A Collection of Unison and Two-part
   Music for Treble or Male Voices. Compiled and edited by Paul
                     Thomas. St. Louis: Concordia, 1957.

Composer	Title
Bach	Beside Thy Manger Here I Stand
Bach	Jesus, Refuge of the Weary
Bach	Let All the Multitudes of Light
Bach	The Only Son from Heaven
Bender	Built on the Rock the Church Doth Stand
Bender	Come, Ye Faithful, Raise the Strain
Bender	O Christ, Thou Lamb of God
Brahms	O Jesus, Joy of Loving Hearts
Bouman	Behold, the Lamb of God
Buxtehude	Arise, Sons of the Kingdom
Buxtehude	To God the Anthem Raising
Franck	Ascended Is Our God and Lord
Greene	Thou Visitest the Earth
Gumpeltzhaimer	Go Ye into All the World
Handel	Daughter of Zion
Lenel	All Praise to God Who Reigns Above
Lenel	Loving Shepherd of the Sheep
Marcello	Oh, Hold Thou Me Up
Mozart	Alleluia
Pachelbel	What God Ordains Is Always Good
Schop	How Lovely Shines the Morning Star
Tunder	Wake, Awake, for Night Is Flying
Vaugh Williams	Unto Him That Loved Us
Vierdanck	Glory to God in the Highest
Willan	Glory Be to God on High
Willan	Holy, Holy, Holy
Wolff	Come, Holy Spirit, Come
Wolff	Sing with Joy, Glad Voices Lift

Renaissance to Baroque. Three Centuries of Choral Music. Selected
   and edited by Lehman Engel. New York: Harold Flammer, Inc.,
                     1962.

Composer	Title
Brihuega	Domingo, Fuese Tu Amiga
	(Domingo, Your Friend Is Gone)
Brudieu	O Jos Claros y Suenos
	(Eyes So Clear, So Calm, So Tender)
Certon	Benedictus from Mass: Regnum Mundi
Des Préz	Ave Verum Corpus
Dowland	Weep No More, Sad Fountains
Dunstable	Quam Pulchra Es
Farmer	Fair Phyllis I Saw
Lasso	Un Jour Ves un Foulon
	(Once I Saw a Fuller)
Monteverdi	Filli Care a Amata

Composer	Title
	(Filli, Fairest and Most Dear)
Nanino	Laetamini in Domino
Palestrina	Congratulamini Nihi
Scheidt	Gib uns heut unser taglich brodt
	(Give Us This Day Our Daily Bread)
Urrede	De Vos i de mi Quexoso
Whythorne	I Have Ere This Time

Chapter VI
Summary, Conclusions and Recommendations for Further Study

In this study, certain historical factors and critical considerations of music for women's voices were investigated and interpreted. These considerations, in turn, prompted speculation about the need for other investigations of a related nature which might be of value.

I. Summary

Statement of the problem. The purposes of this study were (1) to give a brief account of the history of choral singing by women; (2) to establish and validate a set of criteria for selecting outstanding choral works which were originally composed for female or high voices; (3) to annotate each work selected according to the general content of its musical elements and style; (4) to provide catalog-type information which included number of parts, range, publisher, grade of difficulty and type of accompaniment; and (5) to establish and implement a system of multiple cross indexes of those scores examined.

Importance of the study. The growth in the number of women's choral organizations within the last several decades has been significant. The musical leadership of such groups necessarily has involved a great number of men and women who have heretofore had only limited knowledge of the literature for such a vocal combination. Along with this rapid increase in such choral groups, there has been a parallel increase in the number of compositions written for treble choirs by contemporary composers, as well as in the publication of previously inaccessible works by earlier composers. All of these factors underscored the urgent need for a comprehensive bibliography prepared with some degree of discriminating selectivity.

Method of research. Numerous sources were consulted in an effort to ascertain the varying role permitted women in the history of choral performance. This historical investigation provided significant information in at least two ways. First, it disproved a common

163

belief that choral groups comprised solely of women were rare prior
to the nineteenth century and that original music of earlier styles
and composition techniques for this vocal combination was practically
nonexistent. The authentication of choral performance by women prior
to the nineteenth century provided a logical basis to investigate what
music was available to them. Second, it resulted in the discovery of
a substantial body of worthy literature that had been largely ignored.

After determining that a significant body of literature was
available for female choral organizations, a recommended list of
available compositions was compiled and annotated. These compositions were deemed to be of the highest musical quality. To validate
and substantiate the works listed, it was necessary to evolve defensible criteria. The method of research applied to this portion of the
study was an investigation into the nature of esthetics. Pertinent literature dealing with philosophy, esthetics and music criticism was
examined in constructing the criteria employed.

To make this list of maximum value to the conductor search-
ing for appropriate literature, detailed annotations of the works listed under the category of music originally composed for women's
voices were included. Extensive investigation of related topics revealed that there exists no other such annotated bibliography for
music for women's voices. Each work listed was carefully examined
and analyzed. In addition, a substantial number of these works were
heard or conducted in actual performance by various women's choral
organizations at the collegiate level. An approximately equal number
of works "arranged" or "edited" for performance by female voices
was also listed, but not annotated in this study. All of these non-
original works underwent the same critical analysis as the "original"
works and were found to meet the same quality standard. Finally,
a series of indices which provide cross references and category
listings and an index of recommended collections and their contents
were provided.

II. Conclusions

Although the literature available to the mixed choir is more
extensive, the choral literature for all-female choral groups is
neither meager nor inferior. The historical record of female choral

performance reveals that not only has there always been substantial participation in this activity, but that important composers such as Palestrina, Lasso, Pergolesi and Brahms have contributed to the repertoire and were impressed by the quality of such singing in their respective times. Since the nineteenth century, spurred chiefly by the public schools and institutions of higher learning which have fostered choral singing, the number of women's choirs has increased significantly in quantity and quality. This has been reflected in a parallel increase in the number of compositions written for such organizations, many by highly recognized composers.

In attempting to determine a valid set of criteria for a selected list such as that included in this study, the matter of subjective versus objective factors in analysis, response and evaluation was of critical importance. After examining many writings on the subject of esthetics, it was concluded that it is virtually impossible to find agreement in these areas.

Several philosophical and esthetic theories were then examined as an alternate method of developing criteria for selection. It was determined that the most desirable theory for establishing criteria was that of isolationism, which is based on objective analysis and stresses that the most reliable standard of judgment is that determined by the expert in the field. According to this theory, the significance of music is tonal, not extra-musical; the structure of music is the most important criterion for establishing a standard of "good". For these reasons, the theory of isolationism was considered to be the most defensible basis for making the type of value judgments employed in this study.

III. Recommendations for Further Study

The suggestions below indicate some related areas where research or further investigation would be profitable:

1. Similar annotated bibliographies of choral music for male voices.

2. Similar annotated bibliographies of choral music for mixed voices.

3. An annotated bibliography of recommended vocal selections for children.

4. Similar annotated bibliographies of recorded com-
    positions for use in music appreciation or music
    literature courses at high school and collegiate
    levels.

5. Studies to determine how choral program building
    can be made more effective, both for performers
    and audiences.

6. Studies to categorize the specific compositions that
    can be used to develop various vocal skills and
    musical concepts for choral singers.

7. Studies to determine more articulate standards by
    which music may be judged.

8. Addition of selected bibliographies to the state
    music manuals which provide the choice of liter-
    ature for various state festivals and programs.

Bibliography

Books

Apel, Willi. Harvard Dictionary of Music. Cambridge, Harvard University Press, 1960.

Bacon, Ernst. Words on Music. Syracuse, Syracuse University Press, 1960.

Barzun, Jacques. The Pleasures of Music. N. Y., Viking Press, 1960.

Biehl, Herbert. Die Stimmkunst. Leipzig, Kistner and Siegel, 1931.

Birkhoff, George D. Aesthetic Measure. Cambridge, Harvard University Press, 1933.

Buck, Percy C. The Scope of Music. London, Oxford University Press, 1927.

Bukofzer, Manfred. Music in the Baroque Era. N. Y., W. W. Norton, 1947.

Cain, Noble. Choral Music and Its Practice. N. Y., M. Witmark and Sons, 1932.

Chambers, E. K. The Mediaeval Stage. Oxford, Clarendon Press, 1903.

Chaves, Carlos. Musical Thought. Cambridge, Harvard University Press, 1961.

David, Hans (ed.). The Art of Polyphonic Song. N. Y., G. Schirmer, 1940.

Davison, A. T. The Technique of Choral Composition. Cambridge, Harvard University Press, 1945.

Dewey, John. Art as Experience. N. Y., Minton, Balch, 1934.

Dorian, Frederick L. The History of Music in Performance. N. Y., W. W. Norton, 1942.

Drinker, Sophie. Music and Women. N. Y., Coward-McCann, 1948.

Elson, Arthur. Women's Work in Music. Boston, L. C. Page, 1903.

Fellowes, Edmund H. The English Madrigal Composers. London, Oxford University Press, 1921.

Ferguson, Donald. Music as Metaphor. Minneapolis, University of Minnesota Press, 1960.

Fuller-Maitland, J. A. The Consort of Music: A Study of Interpretation and Ensemble. Oxford, Clarendon Press, 1915.

Grout, Donald J. A Short History of Opera. N. Y., Columbia University Press, 1947.

Hanslick, Edward. The Beautiful in Music. Trans. Gustave Cohen. London, Novello, 1885.

Harman, Alec, and Anthony Milner. Man and His Music. 3 vols. Fairlawn, N. J., Essential Books, 1959.

Heyl, Bernard C. New Bearings in Esthetics and Art Criticism. New Haven, Yale University Press, 1943.

Hilpisch, Stephanus. History of Benedictine Nuns. Collegeville, Minn., St. John's Abbey Press, 1958.

Hirt, Charles C. Criteria for the Composing, Arranging and Editing of Choral Literature for the Senior High School Mixed Chorus. Los Angeles, Affiliated Musicians, 1954.

Holst, Imogene. Gustave Holst. London, Oxford University Press, 1938.

Hooker, Edward W. Music as a Part of Female Education. Boston, Marvin Press, 1843.

Jeppesen, Knud. Counterpoint: The Polyphonic Style of the Sixteenth Century. Trans. Glen Haydon. Englewood Cliffs, N. J., Prentice-Hall, 1930.

Julian, Jean. Dictionary of Hymnology. London, John Murray, 1925.

Knapp, J. Merill (ed.). Selected List of Music for Men's Voices. Princeton, Princeton University Press, 1952.

Lang, Paul H. Music in Western Civilization. N. Y., W. W. Norton, 1941.

Langer, Susanne K. Feeling and Form. N. Y., Charles Scribner's Sons, 1953.

Langer, Susanne K. Philosophy in a New Key. Cambridge, Harvard University Press, 1951.

Leichtentritt, Hugo. Music, History and Ideas. Cambridge, Harvard University Press, 1954.

Locke, Arthur W., and Charles K. Fassett (eds.). Selected List of Choruses for Women's Voices. Northampton, Mass., Smith College, 1964.

Manning, Rosemary. From Holst to Britten. London, Worker's Music, 1949.

Meese, Arthur. Choirs and Choral Music. N. Y., Charles Scribner's Sons, 1911.

Mendl, R. W. S. The Soul of Music. London, Rockliff Publishing, 1950.

Meyer, Leonard B. Emotion and Meaning in Music. Chicago, University of Chicago Press, 1956.

Moore, Douglas. From Madrigal to Modern Music. N. Y., W. W. Norton, 1942.

Mueller, John. The American Symphony Orchestra. Bloomington, University of Indiana Press, 1951.

Parker, Dewitt. The Principles of Aesthetics. N. Y., Silver Burdett, 1920.

Rader, Melvin (ed.). A Modern Book of Aesthetics. N. Y., Henry Holt, 1952.

Reese, Gustave. Music in the Middle Ages. N. Y., W. W. Norton, 1954.

Reese, Gustave. Music in the Renaissance. N. Y., W. W. Norton, 1954.

Ritter, Fanny R. Woman as a Musician. N. Y., Edward Schuberth, 1876.

Sachs, Curt. The Wellsprings of Music. The Hague, Netherlands, Martinus Nijhoff, 1962.

Schoen, Max. Art and Beauty. N. Y., MacMillan, 1932.

Scott, Charles Kennedy. Madrigal Singing. London, Oxford University Press, 1931.

Sessions, Roger. The Musical Experience of Composer, Performer, Listener. Princeton, Princeton University Press, 1950.

Strunck, Oliver (ed.). Source Readings in Music History. N. Y., W. W. Norton, 1950.

Thompson, Oscar. Practical Musical Criticism. N. Y., M. Witmark and Sons, 1934.

Thomson, Virgil, The Art of Judging Music. N. Y., Alfred A. Knopf, 1948.

Tovey, Donald F. Vocal Music. Vol. V of Essays in Musical Analysis. 5 vols. London, Oxford University Press, 1937.

Tovey, Donald F. The Main Streams of Art and Other Essays. N. Y., Oxford University Press, 1949.

Trever, Albert A. History of Ancient Civilization. 2 vols. N. Y., Harcourt, Brace, 1939.

Weinstock, Herbert. Music as an Art. N. Y., Harcourt, Brace, 1953.

Young, Karl. The Drama of the Medieval Church. 2 vols. N. Y., Oxford University Press, 1933.

Young, Percy M. The Choral Tradition. London, Hutchinson, 1962.

Publications of Learned Societies and Other Organizations

Broudy, Harry S. "A Realistic Philosophy of Music Education," Basic Concepts in Music Education. Chicago, University of Chicago Press, 1958. Fifty-seventh Yearbook of the National Society for the Study of Education, Part I:62-87.

Christy, Van A. "Evaluation of Choral Music," Contributions to Education, New York, Bureau of Publications, Teachers College, Columbia University, 1948. No. 885.

Mueller, John H. "Music and Education: A Sociological Approach, "
    Basic Concepts in Music Education. Chicago, University of
    Chicago Press, 1958. Fifty-seventh Yearbook of the National
    Society for the Study of Education. Part I:88-122.

Tolhurst, J. B. L. (ed.). The Ordinale and Customary of the Bene-
    dictine Nuns of Barking Abbey. London, Henry Bradshaw So-
    ciety, 1927. LXV. (2 vols.)

                              Periodicals

Bernstein, Leonard. "Speaking of Music, " The Atlantic Monthly.
    Dec. 1957. 104-106.

Bullough, Edward. "Psychical Distance as a Factor in Art and as an
    Aesthetic Principle, " British Journal of Psychology. V:II, pp.
    87-118. 1912.

Dewey, John. "Meaning of Value, " Journal of Philosophy. Feb. 1925.

Reimer, Bennett. "Leonard Meyer's Theory of Value and Greatness
    in Music, " Journal of Research in Music Education. Fall,
    1962. X:2, pp. 87-99.

Schoen, Max. "Psychological Problems in Musical Art, " Journal of
    Research in Music Education. III (1):27-39. Spring, 1955.

Vernon, P. E. "A Method for Measuring Musical Taste, " Journal of
    Applied Psychology. XIV (4):355-362. April, 1930.

                    Essays and Articles in Collections

Angles, Higini. "Gregorian Chant, " New Oxford History of Music.
    Dom Anselem Hughes, ed. Vol. II, Early Medieval Music up to
    1300. New York, Oxford University Press, 1954. pp. 92-127.

Auden, W. H. "Notes on Music and Opera, " The Dyer's Hand and
    Other Essays. N. Y., Random House, 1962. pp. 465-474.

Butler, Samuel. "Note Books, " An Anthology of Music Criticism.
    Compiled by Norman Demuth. London, Eyre and Spottiswoode,
    1947. pp 99-100.

Handschin, Jacques. "Trope, Sequence and Conductus, " New Oxford
    History of Music. Dom Anselem Hughes, ed. Vol. II, Early
    Medieval Music up to 1300. N. Y., Oxford University Press,
    1954. pp. 128-174.

Harrison, Frank. "English Polyphony, " New Oxford History of Music.
    Dom Anselm Hughes, ed. Vol. III, Ars Nova and the Renais-
    sance 1300-1540. N. Y., Oxford University Press, 1954. pp.
    303-348.

Kinkeldey, Otto. "Equal Voices in the a capella Period, " Essays on
    Music. Cambridge, Harvard College, 1957.

Parry, (Sir) Hubert. "The Significance of Monteverdi, " An Anthology
    of Music Criticism, compiled by Norman Demuth. London,
    Eyre and Spottiswoode, 1947. pp. 17-22.

Smoldon, W. L. "Liturgical Drama, " New Oxford History of Music.

Dom Anselm Hughes, ed. Vol. II, Early Medieval Music up to 1300. N. Y., Oxford University Press, 1954. pp. 175-219.

Unpublished Materials

Coffin, Roscoe. "A Handbook of Materials for Choral Programs," Unpublished Ed. D. dissertation, Columbia University, N. Y., 1950.

Bowman, Horace B. "The Castrati Singers and Their Music," Unpublished Ph. D. dissertation. Bloomington, The University of Indiana, 1951.

Johnson, Gerald W. "A Study of Choral Practices and Procedures in Methodist Senior Colleges," Unpublished Mus. A. D. dissertation, Boston University, 1958.

Kingston, Robert J. "A Study of Choral Music Styles Including Current Listing of Available Octavo Music," Unpublished master's thesis, Boston University, 1954.

Schwadron, Abraham. "An Interpretation of Philosophy and Aesthetics for Contemporary Music Education," Unpublished Mus. A. D. dissertation, Boston University, 1962.

Appendix
Key to Abbreviations Used in Chapter IV

A	alto
adapt.	adapted
AJ	Arthur Jordan Choral Series
AMP	Associated Music Publishers, Inc.
APS	A. P. Schmidt
arr	arranger
AST	Arthur S. Talmadge
ATD	Archibald T. Davison
Au	Augener, Ltd.
Bank	Annie Bank
BC	basso continuo
Bir	C. C. Birchard Company
BM	Boston Music Company
BoHa	Boosey and Hawkes
Bourne	Bourne, Inc.
Brodt	Brodt Music Company
CF	Carl Fischer
Ch	J. & W. Chester
Coll	collection
Colombo	Franco Colombo
Con	Concordia Publishing House
Cur	Curwen and Sons
DeRing	DeRing Antwerp
Diff.	difficult
Durand	Durand et Cie
ECS	E. C. Schirmer Music Company
ed.	edited
EHF	Edmund Horace Fellowes
EHG	E. Harold Geer
ELKAN	Elkan-Vogel Company
ESR	E. C. Schirmer, Radcliffe Choral Series
ESV	E. C. Schirmer, Vassar Choral Series
Flammer	Harold Flammer
Galaxy	Galaxy Music Corporation
GB	Gwynn Bement
Gray	H. W. Gray
GS	G. Schirmer Music Company
GWW	G. Wallace Woodworth
HC-L	H. Clough-Leighter
JF	J. Fischer and Brothers
Kalmus	Edwin F. Kalmus
KKD	Katherine K. Davis
LG	Lawson-Gould
Marks	Edward B. Marks Music Corporation
MCD	Music Press, Dessoff Choir Series

Med.	Medium
Mercury	Mercury Music Corporation
Mills	Mills Music, Inc.
MP	Music Press
MR	McLaughlin and Reilly
MS	mezzo-soprano
N	Novello and Company, Ltd.
Ol-Dit	Oliver-Ditson
Orch.	orchestra
Ox	Oxford University Press
P	C. F. Peters
Presser	Theodore Presser Company
Pro-Art	Pro-Art
Remick	Remick Music Company
Rev.	revised
Ric	G. Ricordi
Row	R. D. Row Music Company
S	soprano
SB	Stainer and Bell
Schmidt	Schmidt-Hall and McCreary
Southern	Southern Music Publishers Company, Inc.
Summy	Summy-Birchard Publishing Company
transcr.	transcriber
UPC	University of Pennsylvania Choral Series
Unacc.	unaccompanied
VG	Victoria Glaser
W	M. Witmark and Sons
WGW	W. Gillies Whittaker
WLSM	World Library of Sacred Music
Wood	B. F. Wood

The following diagram illustrates the octave position system employed to designate pitch ranges.

Addresses of Publishers

Arthur Jordan Choral Series, obtain through Marks.

Associated Music Publishers, Inc., 1 West 47th Street, New York
36, N. Y.

A. P. Schmidt, obtain through Schmidt, Hall & McCreary.

Augener, Ltd., London, obtain through Galaxy.

Annie Bank, Amsterdam, obtain through World Library of Sacred
Music.

C. C. Bichard Company, obtain through Summy-Birchard Company.

Boston Music Company, 116 Bolyston Street, Boston, Mass.

Boosey and Hawkes, Oceanside, N. Y.

Bourne, Inc. , 136 West 52nd Street, New York 19, N. Y.

Brodt Music Company, Charlotte, N. C.

Broude Brothers, 56 West 45th Street, New York 36, N. Y.

J. and W. Chester, London, obtain through Marks.

Franco Colombo, 16 West 61st Street, New York 23, N. Y.

Concordia Publishing House, 3558 South Jefferson Avenue, St. Louis 18, Mo.

Curwen and Sons, London, obtain through G. Schirmer.

DeRing Antwerp, obtain through Eklan-Vogel.

Durand et Cie, Paris, obtain through Elkan-Vogel.

Elkan-Vogel Company, 1716 Sansome Street, Philadelphia 3, Penn.

Carl Fischer, 62 Cooper Square, New York 3, N. Y.

J. Fischer and Brothers, Harristown Road, Glen Rock, N. J.

Harold Flammer, 251 West 19th Street, New York, N. Y.

Galaxy Music Corporation, 2121 Broadway, New York 23, N. Y.

H. W. Gray, 159 East 48th Street, New York 17, N. Y.

Lawson-Gould, obtain through G. Schirmer.

Edwin F. Kalmus, 421 West 28th Street, New York 1, N. Y.

Edward B. Marks Music Corporation, 136 West 52nd Street, New York 19, N. Y.

Music Press, obtain through Presser.

Mercury Music Corporation, obtain through Presser.

Mills Music, Inc. , 1619 Broadway, New York, N. Y.

McLaughlin and Reilly Company, 252 Huntington Avenue, Boston, Mass.

Novello and Company, Ltd. , London, obtain through Gray.

Oliver Ditson, obtain through Presser.

Oxford University Press, 147 Fifth Avenue, New York 16, N. Y.

C. F. Peters Corporation, 373 Park Avenue South, New York 16, N. Y.

Theodore Presser Company, Presser Place, Bryn Mawr, Penn.

Pro-Art Publication, 469 Union Avenue, Westbury, Long Island, N. Y.

Remick Music Company, obtain through M. Whitmark.

G. Ricordi, obtain through Colombo.

R. D. Row Music Company, obtain through Boston Music Company.

E. C. Schirmer, 600 Washington Street, Boston, Mass.

G. Schirmer Music Company, 4 East 49th Street, New York 17, N. Y.

Schmidt, Hall & McCreary, 527 Park Avenue, Minneapolis 15, Minn.

Southern Music Publishers Company, Inc., 1619 Boradway, New York 19, N. Y.

Stainer and Bell, obtain through Galaxy.

Summy-Birchard Publishing Company, 1834 Ridge Avenue, Evanston, Ill.

University of Pennsylvania Choral Series, Free Library of Pennsylvania, Logan Square, Philadelphia 3, Penn.

M. Witmark and Sons, 488 Madison Avenue, New York, N. Y.

B. F. Wood, obtain through Mills.

World Library of Sacred Music, 1846 Westwood Avenue, Cincinnati 14, Ohio.

Index